ConnectED Leaders

ConnectED Leaders

Network and Amplify Your Superintendency

Brian Creasman, Bernadine Futrell, and Trish Rubin

ROWMAN & LITTLEFIELD
Lanham • Boulder • New York • London

Some names, events, locales, organizations, and incidents presented in the vignette section are fictitious examples. Any resemblance to actual persons, living or dead or actual events is purely coincidental.

Published by Rowman & Littlefield
An imprint of The Rowman & Littlefield Publishing Group, Inc.
4501 Forbes Boulevard, Suite 200, Lanham, Maryland 20706
www.rowman.com

6 Tinworth Street, London SE11 5AL, United Kingdom

Copyright © 2019 by Brian Creasman, Bernadine Futrell, Trish Rubin

All rights reserved. No part of this book may be reproduced in any form or by any electronic or mechanical means, including information storage and retrieval systems, without written permission from the publisher, except by a reviewer who may quote passages in a review.

British Library Cataloguing in Publication Information Available

Library of Congress Cataloging-in-Publication Data

Names: Creasman, Brian, author. | Futrell, Bernadine, author. | Rubin, Trish, 1952- author.
Title: ConnectED leaders : network and amplify your superintendency / Brian Creasman, Bernadine Futrell, and Trish Rubin.
Description: Lanham, Maryland : Rowman & Littlefield, 2019. | Includes bibliographical references.
Identifiers: LCCN 2018043443 (print) | LCCN 2018055589 (ebook) | ISBN 9781475848496 (electronic) | ISBN 9781475848472 (cloth : alk. paper) | ISBN 9781475848489 (pbk. : alk. paper)
Subjects: LCSH: School superintendents—Professional relationships—United States. | Educational leadership—United States. | School management and organization—United States. | Teacher-administrator relationships—United States. | Communication in education—United States
Classification: LCC LB2831.72 (ebook) | LCC LB2831.72 .C74 2019 (print) | DDC 371.2/011—dc23
LC record available at https://lccn.loc.gov/2018043443

∞™ The paper used in this publication meets the minimum requirements of American National Standard for Information Sciences—Permanence of Paper for Printed Library Materials, ANSI/NISO Z39.48-1992.

Contents

Foreword		vii
Preface		ix
Acknowledgments		xi
Introduction		1
A Superintendent's Call to Action by a True ConnectED Leader		5
1	Foundations for *ConnectED Leaders*	7
	Advice from a ConnectED Superintendent	20
2	Setting the Stage: Humans Disrupted	23
3	AWAKENING: Recognizing the Context for Creating New Networks	39
4	BECOMING: Innovating and Disrupting beyond the Traditional Ivory Tower	55
5	BRANDING: Owning the Image, Promise and Result of a Leadership Networking Brand	73
6	DEEPENING: Inspiring Internal Networks for Community Growth	87
	Intermission: Value-Added *ConnectED Leadership*	103
7	REACHING: Finding Connectivity in Building External Networks	105
8	BELONGING: Supporting Systems and Frameworks That Sustain a Networking Strategy	121

**9 MOBILIZING: Claiming Your Social and Digital Leadership
Networking Presence**   135

Conclusion   149

Afterword   151

ConnectED Advice for Your Journey   153

Appendix: AASA Member Blogs   157

A Final Thought: Chief Networker   159

Bibliography   161

About the Authors   167

Foreword

School district administration is big business. To be effective today, a superintendent must have talents and abilities that extend way beyond the management of curriculum and instruction. You have to be an education thought leader, a politician, a financial wizard, and a best friend to your board members. You have to be an ambassador to the community and an excellent communicator.

Throughout my travels across the country, I often hear the phrase "We can't do it alone" from superintendents. Having been a superintendent for 27 years, I couldn't agree more. It's the most demanding job in America. The challenges can be daunting. No two days are the same. Despite the many challenges our school systems face on a routine basis, scores of school system leaders have stood tall in the face of adversity and have spoken loudly and clearly about the value public education has in our society.

The demands placed on a superintendent's desk are greater than they've ever been. Whether you've been a superintendent for more than 20 years or fewer than 5 years, the nuances, just like in any other business, continue to change.

Public schools are the lifeblood of our democracy and the foundation of our communities. No one can disagree with that. It's gratifying to see the tremendous work being done by school districts on behalf of the more than 50 million students who walk through the doors of our public schools every day. I say "bravo" to the thousands of superintendents and other district administrators who are charged with ensuring that our students are effectively learning and growing in our schools and have successful lives beyond high school.

ConnectED Leaders unpacks some of the critical must-haves for the successful superintendent. More important, any professional, regardless of occupation, would benefit greatly by the hands-on strategies and best practices outlined in the pages of this book that can easily be leveraged in the real-life situations we face on a day-to-day basis.

My colleague Gail Pletnick, former AASA (The School Superintendents Association) president and former superintendent of Arizona's Dysart Unified School District, speaks often about the nation's need to "redefine, redesign and reimagine" teaching and learning environments in our schools to improve the overall quality of our school systems and communities. *ConnectED Leaders* takes a similar approach when it comes to building the model superintendent through such tools as brand enhancement, collaboration, and remaining relevant in the constantly changing landscape we work in.

As we stand at the forefront of this dynamic transformation, it's important that we develop the next generation of leaders. At AASA, for example, we have created a cadre of programs specifically tailored to address how superintendents can grow their respective careers, foster leadership strengths, and develop their skills as school system leaders.

Just three short years ago, AASA provided two professional development opportunities to its members. Today, we have nearly 30 leadership programs available, serving more than 2,000 superintendents and other school district administrators. Professional development like this didn't exist when I was a superintendent. These are truly innovative programs that we're really excited about.

We are purposefully bringing school district leaders together to find out what is working and what is not. It is gratifying to witness true thought leaders of education roll up their sleeves in order to drive change and find the winning solutions so their school districts can succeed. And if their school districts succeed, their students will too.

Through the power of technology, AASA members are expanding their professional learning networks to foster the right conversations about what really matters most to students. To echo the words of Illinois superintendent Mike Lubelfeld, former cochair of AASA's Digital Consortium, our superintendents are creating a "tapestry of learning" for themselves.

Public schools are essential to develop the future generations that will maintain our country's status as a world leader. As we work to reframe the national dialogue around public education and highlight the critical roles public schools play as the bedrock of our civic society, superintendents are working tirelessly to prepare students to be successful, contributing members of their communities.

ConnectED Leaders provides a road map for superintendents to ride a successful journey to excel. Readers of this book are demonstrating a willingness to succeed. Mastering the skills outlined in *ConnectED Leaders* defines what it means to be a "champion for children."

Daniel A. Domenech is the executive director of AASA,
The School Superintendents Association.

Preface

ConnectED Leaders: Network and Amplify Your Superintendency is a book that is long overdue. Futrell, Creasman, and Rubin have done an incredible job of clearly articulating that the superintendency does not need to be a lonely, isolated place. While everyone knows that developing and cultivating communities of support is important, this book very intentionally details the steps that superintendents can implement to create and sustain professional networks.

As you progress through the chapters of this remarkable read, you will learn about the seven stages the authors walk us through in regard to networking and building your personal brand as a superintendent. From **Awakening**—recognizing the context for creating new networks—to **Becoming**—innovating and disrupting beyond the traditional ivory tower—to **Branding**—designing the image, promise, and result of your leadership networking brand—to **Deepening**—inspiring internal networks for community growth—to **Reaching**—finding connectivity in building external networks—to **Belonging**—supporting systems and frameworks that sustain a networking strategy—to **Mobilizing**—claiming your social and digital leadership—this book is a must-read for every superintendent and those aspiring to be a superintendent.

The organization and structure of this book is incredibly impressive. Interweaving stories, quotes, research, and best practice, *ConnectED Leaders: Network and Amplify Your Superintendency* should be a required read in all superintendent preparation course programs. I have read the entire book twice and will be incorporating this publication into the aspiring superintendent and early superintendent certification programs in which I teach. It is my hope that you enjoy this tremendous book as much as I do!!!

Dr. David R. Schuler
Superintendent, Township High School District 214, Illinois
2018 AASA National Superintendent of the Year
Past President AASA (2014–2015)

Acknowledgments

Leading an organization is a complicated process. In many instances, school superintendents today lead billion-dollar organizations and are responsible for the well-being, learning, and success of thousands of students. No matter the size of the community you lead, your work as superintendent, aspiring superintendent, or other system leader is commended and valued.

It comes as no surprise in these complex times for society that the average tenure of superintendents today is fewer than five years. This researched statistic of tenure reveals a lack of stability and sustainability for success. If schools are to be future focused, this fact needs to be addressed. Continuing on this course will have a major impact on student learning. Each day, the support for education continues to decline.

We have a responsibility to push back and to create innovative, engaged, and personalized school communities that restore faith in our abilities to manage education in a changing time. As the Every Student Succeed Act becomes the law of the land and schools face stagnant or declining budgets, we feel it is pertinent to bring a focus on the positive power professional leadership networks (PLNs) have on building educational leadership and organizational performance.

In our opinion and based on our experience, we believe that engaging "PLNs" is a critical practice for any 21st-century educational leader. Filmmaker David Lynch writes of the "chrome optimism" of prior decades. This mood was replaced in the past decades by a skepticism, causing educational organizations to function behind closed doors, isolated and far removed from engaging in messaging. In this world of social and digital transparency, a new world of messaging is shining through and we see those days of distancing are over.

Throughout the book we try to convey the importance of PLNs to the success of *all* students in these changing times. We emphasize that leaders create collaborative leadership constructs not only for their professional growth but also the growth of the entire organization. We encourage leaders to be fearless and creative, empowering themselves as "edge dwelling" leaders on a mission: to grow school networks with the help of internal and external stakeholders for the success of all students.

We bring the power of story to the discussion, using voices of professionals, both educators and business people, whose authentic stories, pertinent information, and creative and practical ideas ignite growth. These voices are what we think makes *ConnectED Leaders* so powerful, relevant, and practical for today's superintendents. Their voices are clear and concise, as if they are sharing with you from across the table, holding a conversation with only you. Listen carefully.

To create PLNs that transform the superintendency and the school district, superintendents and other system leaders must look outside their standard pool of ideas and access new sectors of learning from across the "verticals" of the business world or private sector. CEOs of Fortune 500 companies, business consultants, and small business owners have recognized the value of professional networks as a means of making new contacts, expanding their businesses and increasing sales.

Superintendents can borrow the best ideas from noneducational sectors. We hope that the stories and information presented spur readers to launch an inspiring culture of innovation, a new way of "thinking" when it comes to their own superintendency. PLNs have the potential to spread with viral connectivity in public education. Flex your connecting muscle and seek out the partners from across many industry verticals who want to support schools but may not know how to help you. Lean into teaching them what your school needs.

ConnectED Leaders is the result of numerous and lengthy brainstorming sessions, rough drafts (several is an understatement), and discussions. We ventured into a topic that is not well documented in educational research or in scholarly articles presenting a considerable challenge as we put thought to paper. We relied on our ideas and experiences as networkers, two authors as top educators leading as superintendents, one as a uniquely skilled lifelong educator and business owner, who is comfortable networking at the crossroads of business and education.

We would not have been able to bring this book to fruition if not for the help of many. Honestly, our book took a village to make the literature presentation come alive. This book would not be possible without the chapter "Setting the Stage" written by Ted Fujimoto. His piece is informative, future forward, and expansive in its scope. It is just as inspiring for leaders, as the daily messages he sends out via social media across the world to his more than 100,000 followers.

Ted provided an excellent foundation for thinking big and thinking differently, a vision that we were able to build our message for innovative 21st-century networking leaders. He challenges superintendents to stop being shackled to the status quo and focus on making schools more innovative. Likewise, we are grateful for the "digital principal" and international thought leader and author, Eric Sheninger, for pausing in his busy global schedule to offer his expertise in the area of networking.

Eric Sheninger's writings are always a "call to action" for educators, and his contribution to *ConnectED Leaders* is just that, one that launches the reader's journey through a powerful metaphor and strategy. Another global voice that is a most welcome addition is the voice of Britain's David Price, who in 2009 was made an officer of the British Empire by Her Majesty the Queen for services to education. As senior associate at the Innovation Unit in England, he brings the global perspective, readying our children for a new world of work. In the true spirit of networking, we thank Annalie Killian, vice president of Strategic Partnerships at sparks & honey, who is a valued, featured business voice in our book, for seeing the synergy of David's path with ours and opening the door to connection.

We want to thank Daniel A. Domenech, executive director of AASA, for writing a foreword that spoke to all superintendents and challenged district leaders to reach out and join PLNs. Also we appreciate David Schuler, 2018 AASA superintendent of the year, for providing his valuable PLNs experience as a means to mentor other district leaders to begin networking.

The book concludes with a piece from Morton Sherman, associate executive director of AASA, who provides lasting advice for superintendents embarking on a networking journey. Mort's work is a testimony to the serendipitous power of professional networking as he has a particular "professional glue" that connects all three authors across time and geography: as a supervisor, as a mentor, as a colleague. (We leave the reader to discern which author fits each connection to Dr. Sherman!)

We would be remiss if we failed to mention the contribution of Judy Wilson, former New York City school building administrator, educational consultant, and mentor to New York Public School aspiring principals. Judy's voice and tech-savvy smarts as a digital educator, practitioner, and leader result in her powerfully instructive chapter 9, "Mobilizing," which is a valuable resource guide to the reader and especially to those new to online connection.

We are also fortunate to have Alton Frailey, former AASA president and an experienced educator and superintendent of 33 years. He is a legend among superintendents and was AASA president during which time AASA began to focus on personalizing education for all students. His experience and advocacy in education is unparalleled, and he taking the time to bring this book to print speaks volumes about his dedication to mentorship and servant leadership.

The authors are grateful to AASA's Director of Communication, James Minichello for his insight and guidance on this project. Furthermore, Tom Koerner and Carlie Wall for believing in our book and recognizing the value of networks in education and leadership. The team at Rowman and Littlefield are truly the best in the business. We would also like to recognize three educational leaders who helped to bring valuable, real-world stories to our book. The stories by Dr. Katrice Perera, Dr. Greg Goins, and Dr. Diane Hatchett are powerful. They encourage readers, current and future superintendents, to network and network often. Our book would not have been as useful without their voices and we cannot say thank you enough.

Throughout the book, several superintendents, educational leaders, consultants, business leaders, and world-recognized authors and leaders provided testimonials and words of wisdom that paved our road of meaning, one that will help leaders create a culture of collaboration in their district journeys. We are especially indebted to the thoughtful educators and business voices in our book: John Allen, Rick Jetter, Terry Grier, Susan Hardy Brooks, P. J. Caposey, Marystephanie Corsones, Mike Lubelfield, Nick Polyak, Michael T. Conner, Steve Joel, Gregory C. Hutchings, Jr., Scott Kerr, Todd Daggett, Yee Wan, David Price, Monika Williams Shealey, Christopher Jones, Jeff Kraft, John Stanley, George Calderaro, Sabrina Kizzie, Ying Zhou, Steve Johnson, and so many others who provided testimonials, chapters, amazing quotes, words of encouragement, and endorsements.

Introduction

The ultimate goal of *ConnectED Leaders* is to provide readers with a practical, easy-to-understand text. In a time of many choices and too little time, we want to help superintendents and other system leaders to immediately begin exploring networking engagement opportunities. Understanding professional leadership networks is key to starting the networking journey. Networking is not an event but a continual process of partnerships and strategic, sustained collaboration.

We have identified seven unifying themes for gathering our work. The themes are represented by seven power words, networking principle tags: Awakening, Becoming, Branding, Deepening, Reaching, Belonging, and Mobilizing. At the beginning of each chapter, a quote sets the stage for the reader to recognize the networking principle found in each chapter. Within the chapters, we share our diverse, collaborative experience as authors, educational leaders, advocates, consultants, and K-12 brand specialists. We collectively bring you components and strategies that form the basis for identifying and participating in professional leadership networks.

Our experiences are diverse. Our paths reflect thought leadership from across the nation. No matter the size or location of the school district, professional leadership networks can inform and transform the school district. We aim to guide the educational leader on the path of professional growth.

HOW THE BOOK IS ORGANIZED

Prior to beginning each chapter, we strategically offer a connecting vignette for the reader from a valued, respected voice from the field. Before a superintendent reads one chapter in our book, the authentic, trusted connected voices come to life. We want to spread the word about this style of connecting leadership in a personalized manner. This is how ideas spread—through trusted voices we hear and then tell someone about. Our objective is to help a superintendent understand the benefit of networking through the experiences of real-world educators, superintendents, and business professionals and then to share with others. *ConnectED Leaders* is the first book that focuses on establishing professional leadership networks employing touches of instructive strategies of business to inform practice for superintendents. We want the organization of the book to be as differentiated a text as possible, thus providing a unique experience for the reader and making the journey as connecting as it has been for the authors who collaborated on this mission.

NETWORKING PRINCIPLE: PIVOT TO NEW PRACTICE

The pivot to practice provides the overarching importance of the networking principle or topic for each chapter. The principle is presented in a word and supported in practical terms that explain why networking is critical from each lens and how focusing the principle develops into strategic opportunities for collaboration. Research is included in this section as a means to provide validity to the transformation process. The section includes academic research in a simple and concise format that assists the reader to understand the importance of professional leadership networks.

CONNECTED EDUCATIONAL VIGNETTE

The vignette section provides the reader with a short example of each network principle presented through the eyes of a practitioner. The reader is given a glimpse of professional leadership networks through the lens of short stories, a type of case study of a leadership moment. The best way to gain an understanding of each network principle is to see how superintendents or other educators have created their networks, utilized networks, and actively engaged in networks. In the examples provided, the superintendent and other educational leaders or partners used networks to benefit their growth, not only as a leader, but for the organizational growth of the school district to the benefit of student achievement.

OPERATIONAL ALIGNMENT

Calibrating the experience of bringing networking to your superintendency is focused on aligning the operation of school with the personal and strategic growth of a *ConnectED Leader*. This section grounds our focus in research. According to Hill and Lineback (2011), leaders do not need one but three types of networks: operational, personal, and strategic. We provide the importance of all three in practical terms for school system leaders to understand based on the principle presented in the chapter. Though the terms "operational," "personal," and "strategic" may not be specifically mentioned, each term is part of the fabric of the section.

PAUSING FOR TECHNOLOGY

The section "Pausing for Technology" is a concise snapshot—a reminder of the welcoming world of technology that can spark a network. We offer thoughts and ideas of what is current and practical for leaders as they build tech strategies aligned with each principle presented. This section provides the reader with strategies to use technologies that they can utilize immediately on reading. As many leaders network through social media and as many want to join the tribe, we felt it was relevant and critical to provide a technology section in each chapter to support their growth.

SETTING A PACE: LEADING AS THE SUPERINTENDENT

The section "Leading as Superintendent" provides concrete advice for superintendents and other educational leaders to use as they grow their leadership networks. The advice is aligned with the networking principle and is provided as a means to ignite the urgency to begin to engaging in professional leadership networks. This section's goal is to provide the superintendent and system leaders with the confidence to collaborate in highly strategic partnerships and collaborative opportunities.

SPOTLIGHTING BUSINESS ACUMEN: PRIVATE SECTOR APPLICATION

The section "Private Sector Application" is a favorite section as we introduce the reader to the voices of our business peers who reflect on their private sector networking story so superintendents can relate these business strategies to their role as educational leaders. This section is designed to provide, in a comfortable and friendly way, tools, information, or resources from the private sector that empower superintendents to create, strengthen, and grow their own professional leadership networks.

PIVOTING POINTERS

The section "Pivoting Pointers" is a critical one for several reasons. (1) We believe (through our experience) that we are familiar with each theme to offer our advice to practicing or aspiring school superintendents. (2) We think it is essential for the reader to know and understand the positives and negatives of engaging in professional leadership networks. (3) And we present this section as a summary of each chapter. The section serves as a transition for the reader should the reader desire to read each chapter in sequential order.

A Superintendent's Call to Action by a True ConnectED Leader

Building a network is like taking care of a garden. If you want to get the most out of your plants, consistent attention, watering, and fertilization is needed. Any good gardener knows that you also have to be cognizant of unwanted pests and weeds that can stymie growth and ultimate productivity. These same elements apply when creating a powerful learning network using a combination of traditional and digital means.

Identifying outcomes is the first step. What would you like to get out of your network? How do you see it helping you achieve certain goals? Clear outcomes provide the motivation to continually invest in keeping the network thriving. Over the years I have built what many consider to be an impressive digital network. For me the outcomes come in the form of resources, ideas, strategies, feedback, support, and getting my questions answered. It has to be a two-way street though. I fully realize that others depend on me for not only the same outcomes but other that they have identified to be pivotal to their respective professional growth. Connect with like-minded leaders who will help you meet your specific outcomes.

Consistency is key. For a network to flourish and provide real value, school leaders need to make the time to build and grow their connections. It is not about finding the time but instead making the time. A vibrant network that reaps rewards employs a hybrid approach combining successful communication strategies (listening, body language, eye contact, being present, etc.) with the multifaceted use of digital tools. Successful networkers in the digital age know that to get the most out of connections, one must take advantage of the synergy between old and new school approaches. If you aren't consistent in both, then members of your network will no longer depend on you as a resource.

In addition to giving your network the attention that it needs to flourish, you have to realize that certain components might no longer serve your outcomes. Just like a garden, weeding is necessary every now and again. If a certain social media tool is not working for you, then find another. Same goes with the people in your network. This is about you and your professional growth. If someone you are connected with is not helping you get better, then dump him or her. This is a professional decision, not a personal one. Just always remember that for a network to have value you get what you put into it, and that means keeping it loaded with the best people who will push you to get better.

—Eric Sheninger
Senior Fellow and Digital Thought Leader for the
International Center of Leadership Education
@E_sheninger

Chapter 1

Foundations for *ConnectED Leaders*

CONNECTED LEADERS: AN EXPLANATION

Throughout *ConnectED Leaders*, we try to convey to the reader, superintendents, and other district leaders that by no means is networking transactional or a one-time event. We do not see networking as transactional, and in our opinion, the book shows that for example. In the information presented, the experiences we provide, and real stories of connectivity, the text encourages and supports genuine *ConnectED Leadership* through a social construct of collaboration, peer-to-peer engagement, and a supportive tool of networking.

Networking is specifically about increasing the reach of leaders and the organization, by growing exponentially with intention and a strategy. School leaders are networking to grow, to help others grow professionally, and to grow and transform their organization. But networking also forms critical friendships that all superintendents need, as the superintendency is a lonely and isolated job as created by most district organizational structures. Networking, connecting with other leaders and colleagues, helps to remove silos, or the tendency to work in isolation, that have formed over the years.

Defined, *ConnectED Leaders* is more than just connectivity for the sake of benefiting. When leaders connect with other leaders, rarely is the goal to benefit without reciprocity. For example, many superintendents connect with other superintendents as a means to help coach and mentor, assist others in times of difficulty or hardship, or ignite regional economic or academic growth. The common thread throughout is the formation of lasting friendships, collegiality, and comradery. Networking, connecting with other leaders, specifically, with the sole intention of gaining something professionally or personally, will ultimately lead to failure. Networking must always be a two-way process.

As a superintendent, aspiring superintendent, or another district leader, you have skills and talents that you can share with others in your district, as well as with other external leaders. We try to convey that you should also be networking to share the wealth of your success as a leader so that others will be successful. Offering expertise is not egocentric; instead, it is the realization that coaching and mentorship are at the heart of networking. You are connecting with others as a means to grow a bench full of leaders who will have a lasting impact on public education. What we do today lays the foundation for effectiveness in the profession, more importantly, the success of *all* students in life.

> My evolution from instructional leader to Superintendent has relied heavily on the power of a professional network. My previous work in curriculum, instruction, and new school design was rooted in an 'expertise mindset' and was primarily underscored by data, instructional routines, and research. I knew in order to become a successful change agent in urban education, I needed to adopt a new lens—a 'strategic mindset' grounded in equity and improvement. Exponential growth of this magnitude requires a network that is influential, lateral, and broad.
>
> In August 2017, I matriculated into the prestigious AASA/Howard University National Urban Superintendents Academy. Over the course of the academic year, the Urban Superintendents Academy introduced participants to a range of educational and leadership theories, which challenged me to think boldly about urban reform. Further, the professional network embedded within my cohort provided social capital opportunities to examine best practices to eradicate the status-quo. Having the opportunity to share research and ideas with national practitioners as well as tapping profound experiential knowledge through program mentors was of immense value to my growth as an executive leader.
>
> As I reflect on my first year as Superintendent of Middletown Public Schools, I am proud of my explicit personal and professional growth. Moreover, I am proud to be affiliated with AASA—a coalition that continues to support me through the power of its professional network.
>
> Dr. Michael T. Conner (@DocConner13) Superintendent
Middleton Public Schools, CT

We offer networking as a strategy of supporting resources that has value, especially to those leaders who have never been planful this way about collaboration and connection. We intend to spark the desire to network within the reader in a way that transforms public education in this time of accelerated change. *ConnectED* superintendents are transformative change agents in organizations that are starving for innovation, creativity, personalization, and a culture of collaboration. We argue that networking must be strategic, not accidental, and serendipitous—as the spark of connection eventually fades without tending.

> One of my mentors, Mike Kneale who founded ERDI (Education Research and Development Institute), would make phone calls to superintendents around the country at the most opportune times – moments when they needed to hear a friend telling them to "hang in there." As a former superintendent, he understood the many challenges we faced and how lonely the position was.
>
> He helped me recognize the power of networking and the importance of superintendents sticking together during trying times. As I moved up the ranks, I was invited into influential associations where we continued our learning but, even more importantly, developed lifetime relationships that will endure far beyond my active service. Today, through AASA and other organizations, I continue to understand and believe in the significance of coaching and mentoring leaders. It is a wonderful way to give back to a profession that has meant so much to the future of America – and in turn to America's future leaders.
>
> Dr. Steve Joel
(@sjoel59) Superintendent Lincoln Public Schools, NE

There must always be a purpose, as with anything a leader sets out to do. The support we are offering to people who want to leverage and to leaders who never have been committed to this way of collaboration and connection is to illustrate the power of networks and the activity of strategically building your own unique network.

CONNECTED TESTIMONIALS

> The world is more connected, and knowledge flows faster, than ever before. Education, historically, has been the most private of professions, it cannot be immune, however, from the epidemic of professional peer learning that is transforming the way we live and work. *ConnectED Leaders* offers timely advice to education superintendents seeking to tap into the power of people-powered innovation. Isolation is not an option: for our students, for our teachers and especially for our leaders. Time, however, is at a premium for all leaders. *ConnectED Leaders* will more than repay the time you invest in reading it, whilst simultaneously accelerating your learning, and therefore your impact.
>
> —David Price, OBE
Director, Educational Arts/Cofounder, We Do Things Differently
Author of Education Forward and OPEN

In today's world of education, the only certainty that exists for public school districts is that they will be operating in an environment of constant change—change in federal and state requirements, and change in the learning needs of the increasingly diverse students that walk through their doors. The role of the superintendent is to develop a culture and build the capacity to address this ever changing world without losing sight of the "north star"—that being the success of all students in their district.

As someone who has worked in both public education and the private sector, I have learned how critical professional networking is to be a successful professional. In today's world, district superintendents must develop and hone a myriad of critical skills—self-reflection, collaboration, branding, effective communication—to name a few. Collaboration and networking with colleagues that face the same challenges are key! *ConnectED Leaders* provides readers with a practical guide to build the professional networks and collaborations for superintendents to be successful.

—Marystephanie Corsones
Chief Executive Officer
Collaborative Solutions for Educational Innovation

If you ask any top CEO, whether they are leading a Fortune 500 company or a trail-blazing startup, they will tell you that networking is essential to their success. It's not what you know, but WHO you know. For education's ConnectED Leaders, networking is possibly one of the most valuable ways to build credibility both personally and professionally, and should be viewed as crucial part of your personal brand strategy. And in this brave new world, social media literacy will be an inherent part of your professional networking repertoire.

—Scott Kerr
Principal Strategy and Insights Consultant
Silvertone Consulting

Creasman, Futrell and Rubin offer a refreshing perspective on education branding by highlighting the power of networks and collaboration. Schools across the country are struggling to meet the ever-changing needs of diverse communities with limited resources and supports. By leveraging their partnerships and developing a brand that underscores their commitments and values, school leaders will ensure they are engaged in transformation that results in new networks and positive outcomes.

—Monika Williams Shealey, PhD
Dean and Professor, College of Education
Rowan University

A *CONNECTED LEADER'S* PERSPECTIVE

The superintendency is a very isolated position. Yes, it is high profile and you frequently are in the company of many. Yet, in a very real sense, you are still on your own. Most cannot grasp the continuous delicate dance you must perform.

On one hand you try and keep the focus on the interest of the local community. On the other hand, you have to comply with state and federal mandates that frequently contaminate the context of the work with political interests creating nearly untenable circumstances.

Today's toxic and tribal political environment has weakened the influence of the superintendent in many communities. The voice of the superintendent does not enjoy the high regard or respect of previous years. Additionally, many superintendents are one school board election away from losing a job and possibly career. Networking within a professional association and with friends who are involved with the work helps you maintain perspective and sanity.

—Alton Frailey
Superintendent, Nacogdoches Independent School District, Texas
Past President AASA (2016–2017)

THE WORK OF AASA AS A NETWORK CONNECTOR

Throughout the pages of *ConnectED Leaders* we mention AASA, The School Superintendents Association. Being a superintendent is one of the hardest, most important jobs in America and can make or break public education. For more than 150 years AASA has served school system leaders. The organization has been tirelessly creating networks and helping students to make lasting connections with other practitioners, strategic partners, and what Dr. Morton Sherman, AASA's associate executive director for Leadership Services, refers to as "critical friends."

Since 2015, AASA's Leadership Services Department has convened more than 2,000 educational leaders, who have collaborated and shared model practices for developing and scaling districtwide initiatives in areas such as STEM (science, technology, engineering, and mathematics), personalized learning, early learning, and urban education reform. AASA is the one-stop location for supports and resources for superintendents, aspiring superintendents, assistant superintendents, and retired superintendents.

As a superintendent, professional networking with organizations such as AASA has been a tremendous opportunity to build relationships with top educators across the country as well as push my thinking through courageous conversations about leading issues in education. Building leadership capacity as a superintendent is one of the most important aspects of having a successful tenure. Lifelong learning is essential to being able to effectively lead our school districts across the country and organizations like AASA provide the support and guidance needed to serve young people through vision, integrity and passion. The superintendency is one of the most challenging jobs in the world; however, it is also one of the most rewarding jobs in the world. Your professional network will not only positively influence your decision making as a superintendent; it will afford you an opportunity to establish relationships with fellow superintendents that will last a lifetime.

Dr. Gregory C. Hutchings, Jr. (@DrHutchings)
Superintendent, Alexandria City Public Schools, VA

Every year, at the AASA National Conference, thousands of superintendents from across the nation and around the world converge on a location in the United States to strengthen their practice but more importantly to enrich their networks. In many cases, the national conference is the Super Bowl of networking events for superintendents, as not only do superintendents attend, but so do educational vendors, school board members, partners, and researchers.

Superintendents from across the nation converge at the national conference with a primary goal of learning from their colleagues, friends, and collaborators about the exemplary ideas and practices occurring in education. If you have never had the opportunity to attend, we highly recommend that you make time to attend the national conference, participate in the many networking opportunities, and attend several of the learning sessions scheduled over this multiple-day event.

Though the national conference is the key networking event each year for superintendents, AASA provides several other opportunities to engage in collaboration and form critical networks that can assist superintendents to grow professionally. Each year, AASA offers specific learning leadership programs that are focused on several critical educational topics. We provide a short description as a means to help the reader to grow his or her professional leadership networks.

Each learning cohort is diverse in gender, ethnicity, educational experience, and size of school district. As we mention in our book, diversity in networks strengthens the leader's professional growth, AASA epitomizes the education leader's commitment to diversity. There is a professional learning opportunity for any superintendent to participate and enjoy, and that is why AASA receives strong support from superintendents across the nation. AASA's commitment to professional learning is strengthened through the ongoing continuous improvement of its programs so that learning remains relevant and delivers just-in-time support to critical partners—superintendents, district leaders, and aspiring superintendents.

Our lasting connections with many of the participants who engage in the various leadership development programs that AASA offers for superintendents and aspiring superintendents highlight the importance of each program to the membership. Participants overwhelmingly convey the value of time spent together with colleagues and practitioners learning and growing. Superintendents also cite the chance to engage in networking as important. Through the programs, networks form and expand connection through the common goal of professional growth. We find, through our practice and our research for this book, having a shared goal strengthens the network's potential, resulting in increased engagement.

Over the past years, the leadership team at AASA created a strong focus. Their goal is to help school leaders across the nation face critical issues such as school budgets, teacher turnover, federal policy, the workplace of the future, and more recently school safety—specifically gun violence in schools. The team at AASA is superb at helping school leaders through a combination of strategies to stay strong, and one of the strategies that works is continued connections among critical friends.

When approached by Brian Creasman (coauthor and superintendent), AASA launched a national focus on the emerging needs of rural school superintendents, the largest population of superintendents, to discuss rural issues. AASA continues to bring superintendents to the nation's capital to advocate for public education with national elected leaders. The critical component found through all of AASA's work is supporting school leaders through continuous and ongoing professional learning opportunities that help form a collaborative and diverse network of critical friends that is necessary for leadership success in complex time.

To learn about AASA's many learning and networking opportunities that build capacity, we encourage you to use the following QR code to access AASA's catalog of programs. We would also encourage you to reach out to the many leaders at AASA who are active in many national and international networks. Connect with the people of AASA to access an extensive and expansive network of resources and "critical friends."

THE IMPORTANCE OF PROFESSIONAL LEADERSHIP NETWORKS IN EDUCATION

There are "friend" collectors out there in the digital and social world—those who get a high when their numbers of connections or friends accumulate, escalate, and reach the tens of thousands. We don't really know every connection that we have, personally, but amazing things can happen when you open yourself up to learning more about others using social media, in personal and professional life.

I think my life and identity has transformed because of others because I see the huge potential and value of connecting with others in order to learn from them. What has emerged for me is that I went from having a DLN (daily living network) to a PLN (professional leadership network). I don't share what meal or recipe I just ate while on social media; I share things that others might find useful. I share ideas, reflections, and thoughts alongside others on how to make education more beautiful for students or the world a better place. I'm no longer just a "joiner." I'm committed to helping others and embracing how they can help me to become a better thinker and person.

—Rick Jetter, PhD, is a national education consultant, author, and speaker. He is the cofounder of Pushing Boundaries, LLC, and strives to work on projects that bust the status quo. More about Rick can be found at @RickJetter or at www.rickjetter.com.

Networking is a fundamental necessity for school administrators if they are to successfully move their schools forward in a manner that best serves students and teachers. It allows them to open a broader range of both professional and personal opportunities for growth provided their motivation is not specifically personal gain. As with most interactions in need of a successful outcome, it must be focused on the creation of authentic relationships from which all those involved benefit.

It is important to note that while there are people who network to purposefully obtain a specific result, it is incredibly important to strike a balance by networking to either build stronger relationships that provide greater knowledge and understanding in a specific area or for the gain of others who you serve as a result of your position or purpose. By doing this authentically, the goals you are pursuing or personal improvements you seek will come at a much quicker and personally satisfying pace.

—Dr. Christopher Jones
High School Principal
Whitman-Hanson Regional High School

MEET THE *CONNECTED LEADERS* PLN!

It's our hope that you enjoy the text and that it will lead you to connect with us. In authoring the book, we have started our small PLN as authors and now have grown the PLN through the development of the book and our partners from all over the world! We've written about other's networks. Now we offer you a glimpse into each of our journeys to *ConnectED Leaders*. We look forward to connecting with you but more importantly learning from you through your leadership journey shared with us as members of your trusted PLN.

Brian (Twitter: @fcssuper)

I started my networking during my first year as a superintendent. Being a first-year superintendent in a turnaround school district which was also in a new state, the need to collaborate with other superintendents wasn't optional. I began networking with experienced and first-year superintendents from across Kentucky. In Kentucky, all first-year superintendents are required by law to go through first-year superintendent training.

There were more than 25 new superintendents in 2014, and we all had different backgrounds, experiences, districts, and stories. All of the superintendents in the program, who are still serving as superintendents, have developed a bond so strong that at any time we can pick up the phone and call each other. We periodically share information and strategies by phone, via e-mail, and texting. We enjoy meeting up at the various co-op meetings and state, regional, and national conferences where we regularly talk and catch up, if we have not done so before the gatherings. I was also fortunate to participate in my first year as a superintendent in two national superintendent preparation programs.

The one association that I have gained many new friends from was AASA's National Superintendent's Certification Program. Over the span of two years, the cohort of superintendents from every corner of the United States met several times to grow as leaders. Though we grew professionally through premier learning experiences designed by nationally recognized, veteran, current, and former superintendents, we also developed into a strategic network of colleagues and friends.

Throughout the two years of our certification studies, we grew close, learning about each other's goals, aspirations, families, and troubles. As one of us faced difficulties with district budgets, our school board, or teacher unions, we were able to pick up the phone and access a network of innovative, transformative, and soon-to-be nationally recognized superintendents.

For a first-year superintendent who is an introvert by nature, Kentucky Association of School Administrators' New Superintendent Program and AASA's National Superintendent Certification Program helped me develop the network skills needed, as well as the confidence to engage in a statewide and national network of superintendents who are doing remarkable things for students. Through participating in AASA's National Superintendent Certification Program, I was fortunate to build friendships with many of AASA's staff such as Morton Sherman, Bernadine Futrell (coauthor), Dave Shuler (former AASA president and 2018's national superintendent of the year), and Jay Goldman (editor, *The School Administrator* magazine). All are valuable friends and colleagues to me. As I tell them all the time, I have never reached out to them and not received a response within seconds or a callback promptly.

As a new superintendent, it is so important to have "critical friends", as Mort would say, that are there to help at any time of the day or day of the week. Over the past two years, I was on a team with Bernadine that focused on AASA's efforts to provide support to rural superintendents in the United States. We got to know each other over the year and half of being on the team together. We teamed up again last February at the national conference in Nashville to sit on a conference panel. It is through this panel that we discussed possibly writing a book together about networking.

AASA also provided me a chance to connect with Trish Rubin (coauthor) through writing reviews for book releases. Last year, I reviewed her book *BrandED*. To my surprise, after the review came out in AASA's monthly publication, *The School Administrator*, Trish reached out to me through AASA to thank me for writing such a positive review of her book. In late fall we spoke briefly about writing a book together in the future. Neither one of us expected this goal would be met this soon.

Interestingly, the commonality among your authors is Morton Sherman, who is mentor to all, Bernadine, Trish, and me. Never in my wildest imagination would I have ever thought I would be networking and collaborating on the national stage with rock stars like I am doing right now with Bernadine, Trish, Mort, and so many other friends who are in this book. Not too bad for a kid from Nantahala, North Carolina, a small rural community in the western part of the state.

Bernadine (Twitter: @drfutrell)

Wow, what a remarkable journey it has been to collaborate on this book with the wonderful genius of Brian and Trish. When we first started talking about this work we thought that we would spend time highlighting what others have written in terms of professional relationship development among superintendents. What we did not expect to find was the fact that very few formal guides for networking or connecting were out there for school superintendents. To our surprise, we found many examples in different sectors and roles within education, but very few for school superintendents.

Mort, AASA's associate executive director for leadership services, has always been a trailblazer in this work. During my first year at AASA, Mort asked me to include making time to connect with others who are doing similar work as my professional goal for year one. I was surprised that my boss wanted me to make friends as a professional goal. What came from that was this beautiful reality of effective professional networks for myself. I learned through this process that while inviting someone into your work with a critical lens can be threatening and challenging - it also so rewarding. Really, you can leapfrog years of progress by hearing an alternative perspective about the work. Networking is an essential component of any plan for continuous improvement and I am fortunate to have connected with Brian and Trish on this concept and others.

On a final note about networking, while we were writing this book, I experienced the unexpected loss of my father. I pulled away from everyone and everything, I hid behind text message responses, and took the long way to the elevator so that I would not have to respond to the caring question "How are you doing?". It was this book that reminded me to plug into my network and connections for a recharging. My advice, when it is the hardest to plug into your network, that is when you need to do it the most.

Trish (Twitter: @trishrubin)

I started my love affair with connecting in college. I wanted to be vice president of my sorority but was encouraged to become the membership officer by my "sisters"; in effect, I became "Julie," the cruise director of the Love Boat. I'm a product of 12 years of strict Catholic school education and 4 years in an all-girls' high school. I was a competitive swimmer who logged hours after class in grades three through college, swimming in a solitary sport—face down in a pool lane for hours. I wasn't a born connector.

But I gave up on leading the sorority organization because I discovered I was good at being social. My service jobs in high school and college in the food and beverage industry and in retail helped this shy kid evolve. I became a lifeguard and a swim coach—suddenly I was a "people person." Following college, I was lucky to have a very unique education career. I received media training to work with a program I'd developed for the U.S. Department of Education.

I grew confident in front of people in presentations in the 38 states I conducted PD (Professional Development), which helped me later in my career in central office positions. When I took early retirement to open my first consulting business on getting a master's degree in public administration, my first client was USA Today Education, and it took me on the road to be the face of USA TodayED Literacy. I watched the sales force and learned to pitch into Fortune 500 companies and make connections. I empowered myself further as a member of the National Speakers Association, Toastmasters NYC, and NYC Rotary Club (yes, membership lead again!). These experiences introduced me to superconnected business people whom I watched and learned from for years. It was the National Speakers Association (NSA) who gave me the confidence to write my first book in 90 days—a book about NETWORKING. But it was 2007, and only a glimmer of social media was mentioned in the text—that was important. I learned more face-to-face connecting skills in big rooms full of savvy business people in New York.

My book helped business people network comfortably at events and in business situations. Book in hand, I wound up on the *Today Show*. I learned to talk to everyone in NYC and wound up talking my way into writing cool freelancing gigs and finally to the opening session of the United Nations in 2007 to present to nongovernmental organizations, which sparked my global network. In 2008, I joined Twitter. I was teaching lawyers and financial and tech people about social media online to grow connectivity. I grew my marketing/brand consulting network worldwide due to the success of my first book and traveled to present in Japan and in Europe.

Fortunately, my road led me to Eric Sheninger who became my first coauthor, and I circled back to grow an educator network. Just as I was entertaining the thought of "what's next for me?" Brian Creasman reached out. He knew my work with *BrandED*, and he knew of my original book, *Trish Rubin's New York Minute for Networking*. He persuaded me to join him on his quest to bring the power of networking to superintendents. How could I say no? I describe myself as an educationalist, poised at the intersection of business and education. It was an offer I couldn't refuse.

Keep in mind that my contact with my coauthors has been one of connective trust. We have collaborated together without meeting once in real time! That limitless possibility of connection and trusted networks is what I teach to my clients, my MBA students, even to my own children. I look forward to meeting you online on social platforms—and to the possibility of meeting you face-to-face.

Judy (Twitter: @judywilsonSINY)

It was business as usual for me, a little girl from Brooklyn, New York, to take Sunday trips with my family to visit my Staten Island aunt, uncle, and cousins. But one particular Sunday stands out. It was the day my big cousin Jay, the cousin who always spent time with the little cousins, taught me to play the quite addicting game of dots. Yes, connect the dots. She said the only thing we'd need is a scrap of paper and something to write with.

If you haven't heard of it, Grandparents.com describes Dots as "A griddy" game where dots become lines, lines become squares, and the player with the most squares wins." I didn't realize it at the time, but this game would parallel life in many ways. As a student, I was always connected and involved both in school and after school. But it was in sixth grade, because of my first Spanish language teacher, Mr. John Viverito, that I fell in love with language and knew I wanted to teach and travel. Once I started teaching, I loved my job so much; I raised my hand for everything. I took every chance to network with my school community, always turning dots to lines. I guess I always believed that if you're not connecting and networking, you're not working at all.

Administration was a natural next dot for me to connect. I became a New York City middle school assistant principal in the school where I taught language and later became an elementary school principal. It was somewhere around 2012 when one of my students handed me a copy of *Scholastic Administrator Magazine* entitled "Principal Twitter." That student was Eric Sheninger's son, Nick. He was the messenger. The message was clear. The way to stay relevant in my career as an educator was to become a connected educator. I opened a Twitter account and began growing my PLN. It took some courage, but I also opened a Facebook and Instagram account for my school as well.

As a digital pioneer, Eric was my motivation. By being willing to learn to use 21st-century tools and become a connected educator, my administrative team and I brought many changes and upgrades for the advancement of our entire school community. But a few years later, when I retired as principal, don't think I put my pencil down just because I completed another square. I started looking to connect more dots. I was so fortunate to connect with Trish Rubin on Twitter when *BrandED* was published.

We sparked an amazing professional and personal friendship and have become a "business as unusual" duo. I also currently teach in the School Leadership program at Touro College. I mentor first- and second-year assistant principals for the Executive Leadership Institute at the Council for Supervisors and Administrators in NYC, and I have my own professional development consulting company.

Being a school leader is one tough job. It's intense. And like Dots, if you're too intense or too tense, you'll miss half the squares right in front of you. Therefore, try to relax. Extend your reach and connect with educators globally using 21st-century tools. Don't miss anything. As for me, I'm staying as connected as ever in this next chapter of my life. I hope, by the way, no more scraps of paper and pen are needed to play connect the dots. There's an app for that. Are you up for the challenge? Dots is like life; the more you play, the better you get at it. Stay connected.

Advice from a ConnectED Superintendent
By A. K. Perera, EdD

"You better not fail those kids" is a statement that still motivates me. On my first day of teaching in 1994, my then principal, Mrs. Booker, walked up to me, positioned her face within inches of my own, and uttered that statement, which still serves as my professional mantra. It had only been a week before school was to begin that she invited me to set up a time to what I thought would be to discuss my scheduled student teaching assignment and to meet the master teacher that I would be working with.

Mrs. Booker welcomed me into her office and asked if I thought I was ready to teach full-time. Being a natural competitor, I confidently responded, "Yes!" What she did not know is that I had to put my hands on my knees to keep them from shivering. Mind you, this principal was no stranger but rather one whom I had spoken to on many occasions throughout the previous school year.

While serving as a substitute teacher, I prioritized time to build a professional relationship and to soak in the opportunities to learn from the principal at each school I served. I simply was seeking an opportunity to learn from others, but I unknowingly began building a supportive network that professionally has benefited my career for many years. As I reflect on the opportunities I nurtured, I am positive that the opportunity to teach full time prior to formal student teaching would not have been a possibility.

Since that time and during challenging situations, I have come to realize that if I desire to be an effective education leader in this era of high-stakes accountability, my professional network will always be a key resource. I am sure I do not have to highlight that the not-so-positive national rhetoric and public scrutiny of public education only makes it more difficult for education leaders to be effective without the help of others.

As we are seeing an ever-growing number of students arriving with academic and emotional challenges, the need to partner with external agencies is critical. The impact of global competition on education has created a sense of urgency for the facilitation of 21st-century skills, and so the critical need for leaders to ensure that all students have access to digital learning resources cannot be resolved in isolation.

It's likely not a surprise that how each challenge is dealt with will contribute to the vital success or failure of a school district and the superintendents' overall effectiveness. Undoubtedly, an astute education leader would not attempt to address pressing challenges alone. In this modern technological era, networking that is vital to one's effectiveness should not be solely built through digital resources like e-mail, or text messaging, but rather in a more social format like face-to-face—especially during conferences and seminars.

Professional organizations at the state and national levels offer the best interpersonal opportunities to network and learn from colleagues. Local organizations have a lot to offer, but in my experience, I believe learning from colleagues outside one's district or state fosters creative approaches to problem solving and improved professional development and, ultimately can offer examples of proven instructional leadership approaches. These organizations not only offer a plethora of learning opportunities but are the perfect social, yet professional, setting to begin and to build on relationships with fellow colleagues.

While it is true that my practical experiences revealed the importance of networking, it was my dissertation research in May 2014 that acknowledged my interest in the personal and professional factors impacting female pathways to the superintendency. Why is it that in a profession that is made up of almost 80 percent female most key leadership positions are held by males? Was it a personal choice? Was it the level of responsibility?

What I discovered, among other things, was that females were not willing to allow themselves to be vulnerable to "not knowing" how to do something or they would wait until they had "proven outcomes" to seek career advancements. Adversely, in my dissertation research findings, males possessed more courage or tenacity to seek career advancements without having a proven leadership record, and they consistently sought out networking opportunities through fellow colleagues.

The collected data highlighted the inclination of school boards to hire a male leader with potential leadership effectiveness three times more than they selected a female leader with proven leadership effectiveness. Therefore, one can conclude that the statistical data on the number of male superintendents would be almost three times that of female superintendents.

Dissertation research is not necessary to identify the true value of professional networking. The increased access to a variety of approaches when addressing an issue, emotional support during difficult situations, improved opportunities for professional development, access to proven leadership strategies, or sometimes just a practical understanding of the professional challenges are all reasons to be open to learning from others in any field. The key to finding a good opportunity to network is more accessible than one might think or believe one has time to do.

The options in organizations such as, but not limited to, the AASA, in state education leadership associations, and from education leaders within your region are indispensable. Education seminars, webinars like the EdWeek offerings, workshops like Future Ready Schools, thought leadership sessions through education partnerships, and, in today's hyperconnected world, social media platforms that offer targeted professional chat sessions are making it convenient to professionally network.

Each of the aforementioned opportunities offers not only a variety of networking arenas—they offer professional development for growing new leaders, preferences on the evaluation of programs, researched-based assessment programs, support on dealing with crisis situations, and more—but most importantly opportunities to improve one's leadership effectiveness.

Personally, I have harnessed many learning opportunities to improve my knowledge of personalized learning approaches, mentoring others, utilizing data-informed practices, creating technology implementation plans, goal setting, working and communicating effectively with school boards, sharpening my equity lens, giving the learning community a voice, hiring and retaining effective building leaders, and, more recently, shaping state and national education legislation and policy.

I am especially proud of the fact that I was able to expand my professional network from coast to coast and with colleagues leading in large urban districts of 200,000 or more students to small rural school districts of 2,000 or less students, as a result of acquiring a national certification through AASA in 2016. No matter the size of the school district, the geographical area, or the makeup of the student population, when it comes to teaching and learning, the work of an education leader has to be exhibited every day, in every school, and on behalf of every student—no excuses.

In the field of education leadership and due to the complicated nature of serving a community of learners, one is required to work with and alongside others; but as in any field, connecting and learning from others is always a personal choice. With that said, I will affirm that all that I am and hope to be in the field of education leadership is the result of conscious decisions to build and nurture professional relationships through interpersonal networking. As a devoted education leader with the personal belief of having morale, an imperative to never fail kids, I will always seek the knowledge and wisdom of colleagues in my professional networks and am willing to offer the same support.

Chapter 2

Setting the Stage: Humans Disrupted

E. Ted Fujimoto

Sometimes a date becomes historic. On January 9, 2007, at the Macworld conference, Steve Jobs introduced the iPhone to the world. Until this point, the public had yet to be convinced that watching videos and using the Internet on your phone was remotely a good idea. This announcement was only the beginning of a cascade of technologies that would change our lives.

Later that month, Netflix announced its streaming video service. It's hard to believe that when then senator Barack Obama launched his campaign that year, social media had just started to reach the public, and there were fewer than 5 million Twitter users in the United States. Services we have now come to know as Uber, Lyft, Airbnb, Snapchat, Instagram, Dropbox, Kickstarter, Hulu, Pinterest, Tesla, or Spotify did not exist yet—they would arise a few years later.

Looking back, while technology and apps received a lot of attention, it's not the most important story. Neither was pervasive access to information because the Internet had been already in heavy use more than 10 years. What has changed in society from 2007 is how people are able to connect with each other today in more ways than ever before—crossing geographies, time, and social circles.

I'm able to maintain closer personal and professional relationships with a greater number of people, which would have been impossible before. We can see real time what is going on in another part of the world during crisis and unrest through the eyes of an ordinary citizen versus relying exclusively on the filter of only a few number of news reporters.

People representing themselves or people representing organizations can connect and interact with a large number of people more frequently and less formally than ever before at nearly zero cost. I call this the "democratization of relationships." Most structures of organizations and entire sectors were built on a hierarchical structure and factory mentality that are challenged at their core because of democratization of relationships phenomenon.

Some organizations are able to embrace it, use it to innovate rapidly, and bravely pivot to meet the changing needs and desires of their customers. What comes to mind is Netflix pivoting from mailing DVDs to streaming with building machine learning intelligence that knows the viewing habits and tastes of its customers more than any other media company. In other organizations, the democratization of relationships is considered a toxin that undermines their structures of rule and order and comfortable way of doing things, like taxicab companies and Blockbuster.

This is a lot of change that feels reminiscent of other shifts we have seen during our lifetime, but this is different both in the magnitude of change and how it will impact us as humans. The industrial revolution happened during a 60- to 80-year period of time. The transportation revolution occurred over a 30-year period of time. Over the next seven years, I believe we will see more profound changes 10 times greater than we have in the past 20 years.

These developments will bring to question even our role as humans in society and how we contribute to it. Our society is not actually equipped for it. Most industries are not prepared. Our education system may be the least prepared of all—operating in slow motion as the world around it is moving in time lapse and accelerating faster and faster.

Throughout our lifetimes, we have already experienced periods of technology and societal innovation from personal computing, the Internet, mobile phones, social media, and electric cars—so why is this different now? This is different because, for the first time, machines are starting to learn, replicate, and improve on certain technical skills faster and better than humans. This is not a futurist pipe dream but a fast-emerging reality in many sectors.

What made this possible now versus 10 years ago is that there is enough CPU power to conduct machine learning/artificial intelligence at scale and high availability of cloud-based computing and high-speed wireless data connectivity. This is similar to if someone told you back in 1990 what the impact of mobile, the Internet, and social media will be 20 years later; it would be hard to imagine—even though now it seems so obvious.

We, even young kids, expect to be able to connect to "our" data and information anywhere. In this evolution, machines are generating their own intelligence. We already know nearly all credit card fraud detection and loan applications are processed nearly entirely using artificial intelligence. These two additional examples that already exist will give you a taste of what is coming.

The first example is a Montreal-based company called LANDR. If you are a musician and you record a song, the typical process is that you would have to send it to an audio engineer to get it mastered in order to use their magic and make it sound right. You will probably pay thousands of dollars to get this done. There are some legendary audio engineers who will cost you a lot more.

Using machine learning, LANDR's machines analyzed over 2 million songs, both pre-master and post-master, and learned the nuances of audio mastering techniques and even the unique approaches of certain legendary audio engineers. Some musicians and industry-respected audio engineers I've spoken with say that the LANDR machine learning got them 90–100 percent of the end result they were seeking. For as low as $4 per month, you can upload your song to LANDR and get it mastered.

The second example is Ultromics from Oxford, England. Using machine learning from analyzing thousands of echocardiogram images, the system is able to diagnose coronary heart disease with more accuracy than physicians more than 80 percent of the time. When the system is used together with a physician, the diagnosis improves by 90 percent compared to physicians without the system.

I wonder how the skills and role of physicians need to shift if machines become actually better at performing technical skills than what physicians can perform. The role and needed skills of humans is an important question many professions and sectors will need to answer in this new era.

The notion that sectors have been disrupted before is clichéd because disruption at some point is inevitable and unavoidable. Entrepreneurs speak of "disruption" and "innovation" as almost synonymous and as a good thing—a badge of honor to make their mark that will supposedly make them and their investors lots of money. Even the education sector has experienced various types of disruption in the school choice movement with charter schools and vouchers, for example. However, there can be a dark side of disruption.

Disruption can be exactly that—disruption that devolves into utter chaos. Well-functioning sectors can be destructively disrupted when equity is not valued. The music industry is a case of destructive disruption where streaming services set royalty rates in a way that a musician would have to stream to all of Europe to make a minimum wage equivalent.

Disruption is always messy. It can end up being fatal to an organization if the organization is not prepared (Blockbuster), or it can be constructive to help the organization evolve in a healthy way (Netflix). It is especially messy because we are seeing two major shifts occurring simultaneously: democratization of relationships and the machine learning era.

In light of this, there are important implications for our education system to stay relevant. What should students really be learning, especially if they can look up pretty much anything online and the vast majority of technical skills will be handled better by machines than humans? How quickly does our education system have to be redesigned to stay relevant? It took more than 20 years just to get the practical project-based learning methods to be generally recognized in schools. We can start to unpack these important questions by understanding potential new roles for humans and what humans will be doing less of during this period of change.

NEW ROLES FOR HUMANS

Not only are machines starting to learn, replicate, and improve on certain technical skills faster and better than humans, but perhaps for the first time in human history, technology is closing in on having capabilities that outstrip our ability to adapt to it. This is especially true in areas where machines will no longer need to operate and behave from specific human direction and programing. Machines are entering the beginning of an era where they operate on accumulated self-learning that surpasses our own abilities to analyze and learn certain things.

As machines build on their capabilities, I have tremendous confidence in our fundamental ability as humans to adapt toward a higher order of skills that are unattainable by machines and giving up to machines the mundane to highly technical tasks better suited for them. This could actually be freeing and refreshing and not scary. Individuals who can make this adaptation quickly will thrive, and for those who don't—well—it will be tremendously painful. The education system needs to do a better job in helping students make this adaptation.

A fair amount of focus in many schools over the past 20 years has been around how to help students develop 21st-century skills. While the headline skills make sense as a basic definition (communication, collaboration, critical thinking, creativity, etc.), it is not enough. In many circumstances, machines are better communicators and collaborators (i.e., notifying you of a credit card fraud alert and helping you resolve it). In certain circumstances, machines may end up making better judgment calls than humans (e.g., driving a car or examining heart imaging). We need to push to a higher level of skills that machines cannot do.

Here are a few possibilities of redefining these skills toward that higher level that are uniquely human:

1. *Empathy.* Humans can recognize and act on with care and concern for the emotional and physical well-being of other humans, themselves, and other living things.
2. *Relationships.* Forming strong, healthy, and productive professional and/or personal relationships with other people and developing a deep understanding of them and their abilities and challenges.
3. *Leadership.* Bringing the right people together and forming an environment that engages them to work together to reach common goals.

4. *Communication.* Communications using design, methods, and tools that shape another person's thinking, perspective, and actions.
5. *Systems thinking.* Understanding, designing, and redesigning the optimum organization of people and machines and how they work together from end to end toward a desired purpose and result.
6. *Creativity.* The ability to create, reorganize, and/or express ideas and ways of doing things in an unexpected positive way and finding challenges and problems to solve that provide additional opportunities.
7. *Critical thinking.* Discerning the quality and importance of information and knowledge, understanding gaps between knowledge and skills and developing methods to close them, understanding risks and limitations, and stress testing ideas and products.
8. *Learning.* Providing experiences and implementing processes that permanently widen and deepen a person's and/or machine's perspective, understanding, and skills.

People cannot develop these skills by themselves in isolation. Learning these skills takes more frequent and more sophisticated interactions with other people. Organizations can benefit when they intentionally support and promote these interactions both internally and externally at all levels.

POWER OF NETWORKS

Landmark examples exist of how high-performing transformative organizations have leveraged the power of networks to execute with excellence, being nimble, making uncomfortable pivots, and staying focused on their mission. In the 1980s, the automobile dealers were in a crisis spiral. According to Harmon (1992), in the United States alone, more than 300 types of cars and 200 truck models were being offered to customers.

This meant customers had more choices on what vehicles they purchased and where they purchased vehicles. Improved product design and manufacturing had made cars more reliable, which directly cut into the service revenues that drove most of the dealers' profit. As dealers fought over market share and declining profits, many resorted to desperate measures to win sales through sleazy sales floor tactics and games.

It was not long before dealers became rated as one of the most hated sectors in customer satisfaction by consumers to the point it was tarnishing the automobile brands themselves. Some of the automobile brands had plans to introduce new lines, including in the luxury segment, like Acura from Honda, Lexus from Toyota, and Infinity from Nissan in addition to Saturn as General Motor's big experiment.

Launching these brands with the broken retail experience would have compromised hope of success. This began the process of redesigning the retail network experience for customers to look and act completely differently than decades of bad habits baked into the norm of how auto dealers operated.

According to the National Automobile Dealers Association (2018), Twenty Groups, a professional leadership network sponsored by the automobile brands along with automobile dealer trade associations, was one of the pillars of practice that, I believe, became the underpinning to manage this transformation across thousands of independently operated auto dealers to redesign and sustain a promised customer experience.

Twenty noncompetitive dealer peers were matched from across the country based on similar markets served. Participation was often mandatory. Discussions were confidential, which encouraged more openness in interactions and information sharing. The group of 20 dealers met in person three to four times per year for one-and-a-half days to three half-day sessions and via teleconference every month for an hour or two.

Monthly, dashboard results were shared with all group peers, which covered a gamut of indicators from financial performance to customer satisfaction. Each session was carefully aided by a certified Twenty Group facilitator using a well-defined protocol. The focus of the sessions was to surface outlier positive and negative performance results in specific areas and to help dealers in their understanding of the underlying environment and practices that were driving this performance.

Collaboration protocols were used to help dealers learn about and implement specific practices that could benefit their own performance. This process enabled the large two-thirds majority of dealers in the middle with average performance to become better and learn how to recognize and prevent slippage into the bottom third. Top-third performers received peer and auto brand organization recognition and reinforcement, which made it easier for them to sustain those "winning" practices within the dealership, often running counter to the traditional way of doing things.

The number of 20 people in a group was not by accident. Any larger, the deepness of relationship building and sharing would start to become shallower and limited by time. Too small, the experience base to build from becomes narrower and also becomes economically more expensive. With 20 people, one can learn from 19 other dealers, and every hour of collaboration time offers each participant up to three minutes of space.

Professional leadership networks are not exclusive to collaboration with other peer organizations. It is powerful for use for collaboration within the organization at any level and with any combination of teams. It was critical to the success of Ritz-Carlton's rapid global expansion, which at one point in its history doubled the number of properties to 73 in many new countries within 10 years.

Numerous locations were places where Ritz-Carlton was the first five-star property. It had to recruit its team members from the existing workforce with little hotel experience—let alone a five-star hotel experience. In some cases, its hotel workforce lived in huts—literally. Its challenge was how to deliver a world-class, five-star experience and mind-set every time from guest one on day one across all its properties. In many ways, all five-star hotels have basically the same operating functions and similar buildings. The consistent execution of delivering a five-star, world-class experience to each and every customer was the only differentiator between five-star properties.

To accomplish this, Ritz-Carlton established its legendary gold standard, "We are ladies and gentlemen serving ladies and gentlemen." It is more than a tagline. It is not a task or a procedure but a way of thinking that drove all team members' motivations and actions. According to The Ritz-Carlton Leadership Center's Blog (2014), to reinforce this mind-set of "ladies and gentlemen serving ladies and gentlemen," Ritz-Carlton has a mandatory nonnegotiable "Daily Line-Up" for at least 15 minutes each day at the beginning of each shift for each team.

At the Daily Line-Up, the team has an opportunity to recalibrate around an element of "ladies and gentlemen serving ladies and gentlemen," including a celebration of how they individually and as a team exemplified this culture and reflected on how they individually and as a team could further improve. Exemplary stories that came from other teams from its property or other properties worldwide may also be shared.

This powerful practice ensures that every day each Ritz-Carlton team member is able to get into the right mind-set and strengthen relationships with teammates before interacting with his or her first guest. Another benefit is that Ritz-Carlton does not need to micro-manage and inspect for behavior—truly empowering its team members to use their best judgment to serve their guests. According to Bailey (2017), employee turnover at the Ritz-Carlton is less than 20 percent compared to the typical more than 50 percent turnover in five properties—creating a more stable and sustainable environment.

In the education sector, there are some great examples of similar use of professional leadership networks like Twenty Groups and Ritz-Carlton's Daily Line-Up. New Tech Network and Big Picture school design networks with over 200 schools each have a "Meeting of the Minds" that are structured nearly identically to Twenty Groups. At a school level, both students and staff first period advisories operate in a similar fashion to the Daily Line-Up, with the mind-set focused on strengthening the relationship culture of trust, respect, and responsibility and attending to each other's social-emotional needs.

The similarities are not by coincidence. New Tech Network and Big Picture Learning replication system at the beginning were informed directly by the groundbreaking work executed within 11 automotive and hospitality retail network redesigns facilitated by Deiss Group, who happened to be a client of mine during the 1990s.

The amount of pivoting and transformation that institutions must go through to come even close to delivering on the promise of "preparing students for the 21st century" is sobering. The typical hierarchical decision-making depends too much on the limited abilities of even the most competent educational leaders to understand enough of the dimensions of how the world is changing to make well-informed decisions.

On top of this, many of largest stakeholders in education as well as regulators are barely comprehending and are unprepared for the level of change in society that is already occurring. I believe professional leadership networks are the most important practice to all sustained organizational transformation and its ability to pivot through the most critical moments in this transformation, and it is essential to replicate and sustain the transformation. To support this type of organization, the very definition and practices of what it means to be a leader will also need to be redesigned.

FIVE PIVOTS FOR EDUCATIONAL LEADERS

I believe there are five pivots that educational leaders need to make in how they lead. While these will not by themselves be all the magic bullets, without them, it will be impossible to pivot your organization successfully and in the right time frame.

Leadership Pivot 1: Create Routine Calibration Experiences and Inspect a Lot Less

Leaders should become experts in curating and delivering calibration experiences for their stakeholders, including their leadership teams, school board, teachers, and community members. By doing so, they can spend a lot less energy and time managing performance by inspection. A worthwhile calibration experience for an individual or a team is one that because of what they experience, their perspective is profoundly changed permanently. They cannot go back to thinking or acting as they did before. This is a high bar.

For calibration experiences to work effectively, they must (1) be routine with specific time and locations baked into the calendar; (2) have the right mix of participant stakeholders, decision makers, and influences, where the collective experience creates alignment; (3) use good protocols for facilitation; (4) be experiential with firsthand experiences and dialog with actual practitioners; and (5) be frequent enough to build strong relationships and expertise between participants and practitioners.

Here is an example: In their more than 20-year history, New Tech Network and Big Picture Learning have been experiencing a growing interest by communities and whole districts looking to improve 21st-century skills outcomes with their students. Most of New Tech Network and Big Picture Learning schools were started because at the beginning, a community group of 25–50 people representing a roughly equal mix of educators, community, business, civic, and school board members spent a day at a demonstration site of at least two school designs for an in-depth study of the design. This has been initiated by any combination of school district, school board, policy makers, civic leaders, business groups, or other community leaders.

On these demonstration site study visits, for the first time, they had a collective shared experience for a high-functioning, 21st-century learning environment that they had only spoken about in terms of goals, aspirations, and theory. It is important to note that what they saw was not a one-off example of a small set of interesting practices. They experienced schools that have implemented with fidelity a set of fundamental replicable practices that form a whole-school design and were part of a support system to help replicate the design.

I've witnessed time and again a profound transformation of thinking, insight, and engagement of groups within one day. Teams and stakeholders involved in this work should never try to make decisions with only theoretical knowledge and goals. They must commit to experience firsthand the very best implementations in the country or the world doing school-wide or district-wide, project-based learning that delivers results on 21st-century skills outcomes before making these decisions.

While these may seem like a lot of up-front work, in the end it is a huge time and energy saver that results in better decisions. Decisions start to flow in a month-to-month fashion versus multiple years. Without these calibration experiences, it is like a city commission trying to approve a five-star hotel property for development on an undeveloped island whose personal and professional experience has been only with one-star motels and who have never stayed at a five-star property.

A school-level example of calibration follows. Many schools practice a daily equivalent of Ritz-Carlton's Daily Line-Up at the beginning of each day for the school team and a first period advisory for students. A common mistake some schools make is allocating too little time and/or including too many people as part of the process. For example, 25 people with a 10-minute period gives each participant only 24 seconds, which is completely insufficient for meaningful connection and calibration. Think about how much time is truly needed to ensure each participant has sufficient time to strengthen relationships with teammates and to share and receive.

As educational leaders, think about how each of your school or district team members as well as your board members could be guaranteed a certain number of type of calibration experiences throughout the year that are directly related to the work at hand and shape the view of work needed for the future.

Consider having (1) external calibration experiences around the country twice per year for board members, principals, teacher leaders, and rotations among select teachers; (2) video conference conversations with external practitioners every other month; (3) interorganizational calibration experiences between schools at least twice per month; (4) intraschool calibration weekly across interdisciplinary teams; and (5) school-level calibration on culture for both adults and students at the beginning of each day.

When you create more calibration experiences, the magic starts to happen that you will need to spend a lot less energy and time trying to improve the performance of your teams by inspection. Ritz-Carlton's "ladies and gentlemen serving ladies and gentlemen" mind-set is calibrated through the Daily Line-Up and eliminates the need for what is known by some in the industry as "smile policies" that dictate step-by-step behavior about how to be "friendly."

Even with lots of inspections and silent shoppers, the "smile policies" approach resulted in inauthentic interactions that guests could distinguish easily and lots of failures that inspections could not possibly uncover until too late. Think about all the inspections you and your team are conducting to try to change outcomes of behavior and replace them with calibration experiences that focus on shifting mind-set.

Leadership Pivot 2: Set Team Culture to Do What Is Right—Not What Is Comfortable

Every failed or underperforming organization throughout history has one thing in common: it failed to make uncomfortable decisions required to pivot its organization and regressed into the "comfort zone." I believe this is a structural flaw and not by intention of the organization's leaders. No leader went to work thinking he or she wanted to make the organization fail.

In education, there is so much in the organizational design and culture about "compromise" and agreement. I have been privy to the inside workings of more than 100 failing schools that ultimately closed. They also had one thing in common—the inability to make the hard decisions and many times even the basic ones. I wonder how many education transformation initiative efforts are structurally doomed from the regression to the comfort zone bias.

The structural flaw is that for any given issue that needs to be solved by a team, each team member has bias and too much focus is placed on coming to a solution that each team member can "live" with. The emphasis should be about what decision is right for the future of the organization and its customers regardless of how uncomfortable it is. Here are some things to consider doing as an education leader to avoid the comfort zone bias in the work of your teams:

1. At the beginning of each strategic meeting, intentionally call out and discuss the danger of the "regression to the comfort zone."
2. When possible, establish a safe zone for team members. Establish and communicate guiding principles ensuring that the individuals' future is safe as long as they are willing to pivot their own skills and leadership style. At the end of each session, have team members reflect how they may need to personally pivot their skills and leadership style—what they need to do more of, less of, or differently.
3. Obtain verbal agreement from each team member that they are committed to focusing on what is right for the future of the organization and students regardless of how uncomfortable it is.
4. Balance discussion between what pivots the organization must do to survive the future and what the consequences are to the organization that fails to pivot enough or pivot at all.
5. Use calibration experiences to make real the changes that are happening in the world as well as the opportunities and consequences of inaction or not enough action, for example, talking with the most successful and fastest-growing company leaders in your region and visiting their companies to understand work environments.

Leadership Pivot 3: Create and Maintain Your Freshwater Tank

It is one thing to have motivated bright teams that want to do the right thing. It is another to ensure that your organization's systems are in alignment to support doing the right thing. I've witnessed so many unintentional ways an organization's system and policies are directly toxic to the very thing that everyone has agreed is the right thing to do.

One example I have frequently observed in many school districts is the huge disconnect between their initiatives and commitment to provide students "personalization" based on students' needs and the inability to get rid of the mandatory district wide curriculum pacing guide. A district wide curriculum pacing guide is the antithesis of any notion of any personalization.

For a team tasked to pivot and innovate is much like being a freshwater fish dumped into a saltwater tank. Some fish are stronger than others and outlast. But, eventually, they all succumb to the salinity of the water and die, or they must leave the environment or profession. It is not enough to have the right intention and try to do the right thing—just like intentions and righteousness are not enough for a freshwater fish to survive in a saltwater tank. As an education leader, you must define precisely and help implement the ecosystem needed for the effort to thrive and sustain.

Another example of what would seem to be an innocuous, well-intentioned district policy that was encountered in schools in the New Tech Network was a district's mandatory district wide professional development that was scheduled at the same time as the New Tech Network's national new school's professional development. Although the district had strong commitments to implement the New Tech Network school design, its policy and schedule conflict would seriously compromise the school's ability to launch with high fidelity.

Fortunately, last-minute waivers were granted in most cases after much negotiation between the school team and district and ultimately the school board. Why should a school team have to negotiate for something so basic that was technically already committed to by the school and district teams?

Consider that for each transformative initiative approved, it required that the team inventory all district- and board-level policies from end to end and categorize them as neutral, helpful, or hurtful to the initiative. I have found many school-level teams are not very familiar with the actual district policies and may need direct support to help them do some of the initial legwork and walk through these policies. Perform a quarterly review with the team to see if there are others that need to be waived or created as the result of their learning and experience.

You will want these waivers and board policies as superintendent turnover proof and board turnover proof. Therefore, it helps that these policies and waivers are passed by the school board and worded to ensure that when and if there is a conflict between existing or new district or board policies, these take automatic precedence and that these do not expire unless board action is taken otherwise. Sophisticated districts have also used similar processes to work with state- and federal-level policies.

Leadership Pivot 4: Use Technology Wisely to Empower Humans

Invest in technologies that will free up your team members to focus on higher-order thinking and leadership. A good place to start is surveying team members to identify manual technical tasks performed routinely that take up to 10 hours or more of their work time per month—which is more than 5 percent of their work time. Seek out opportunities to simplify approval processes while maintaining necessary controls. Some illustrations of technology use that can save 5 percent or more of a team member's time follow:

- Eliminating manual signatures on documents and having all documents being delivered and signed electronically, especially purchase order approval processes.
- Employee expense reports and reimbursement—make it all online with the ability to capture receipts via smartphone and eliminate the physical receipt requirement. Consider moving up threshold to require a receipt where practical. One organization we worked with found that just by increasing the receipt requirement threshold by $5.00, it reduced the amount of time spent capturing and processing receipts by 25 percent.
- Ban PowerPoint presentations. Just like Jeff Bezos at Amazon did, ban PowerPoint presentations and replace with a one- to six-page memo that everyone reads to themselves prior to or at the beginning of meetings and before entering discussions (Gallo, 2018).
- Ban e-mail for internal communications (Vozza, 2015). Replace with online discussion forums and real-time collaboration tools (e.g., Slack) as well as with more frequent but shorter well-constructed collaboration sessions (in-person or virtual).
- Simplify and reduce reports—have each team identify all data reports being prepared and categorize them as follows: (a) we cannot function effectively without them, (b) we don't use them much; and then everything else falls into (c) we probably don't need them. Eliminate all of (c), have (b) only prepared when needed, and have (a) completely automated when possible in preparation and distribution.

Leadership Pivot 5: Set the Pace for Change

Even when organizations tried to pivot, many failed to pivot fast enough. The inability to change due to the lack of preparedness is not an excuse and will not prevent organizational failure. In addition, pivoting when the organization is not prepared simply makes the organization fail faster. This chicken or egg situation makes setting the pace for change a bit of a tricky equation. In this equation, there are some constants to work from. First, the changing world waits for no one.

This begs some interesting questions for educators. What higher-order skills will our students entering the workforce over the next 10 years (students who are possibly in elementary school now) need? Are the technical skills or even some basic skills we are teaching them going to be sufficient, at the right level or even relevant in this new reality? What and by when do we need to make fundamental changes in how and what we teach in time to deliver the promise of preparing students for their world?

Another constant is that an organization cannot maintain two different competing cultures. Odds are in the favor of the older dominant because as an incumbent it is already and better supported by the existing system. The new culture is like the freshwater fish. This is why it is so important to make the systems change to support the new culture and, I would add, make the system toxic to the old culture.

I often hear how organizations rationalize implementing transformation incrementally. I believe this is too often a cover for what is really happening—regressing to the comfort zone. Of the organization transformations I have observed that have been the most successful, in each there was an intentional and stated deadline for the pivot, and it was done as quickly as possible—sometimes within one year. One common retrospective sentiment I hear from superintendents conducting the transformation of their district's cultures is that they wish they had shortened the time frame and that they underestimated the energy required to support the two competing systems.

PUTTING IT TOGETHER

Over the next 7 years, we will see more profound changes at 10 times magnitude than we have in the past 20 years. Technology will give us more and deeper opportunities and methods to connect (democratization of relationships) with each other while through machine learning we become better at taking technical tasks off our plates.

Rapid changes in technology will bring to question even our role as humans in society and how we contribute to it. In preparation for our new role as humans, education at all levels needs to focus more on building higher-order thinking skills (empathy, relationships, leadership, communication, systems thinking, creativity, critical thinking, and learning) and less on the technical.

Technical skills are becoming more proprietary and specialized that only the companies that employ them are in a position to help people learn them. Our organizational structures and roles of leadership must shift to leverage the opportunities created by the democratization of relationships; otherwise, organizations that are not able to adapt will lose their relevance. It is concerning that our education system is operating in slow motion as the world around it is moving in time lapse and accelerating faster.

Education leaders can help transform and pivot their organizations by leveraging the power of internal and external professional leadership networks and by pivoting how they lead. The five imperative pivots education leaders must make to be effective in this new era follow:

1) Shift most of the time spent in performance management on curating calibration experiences and a lot less time on inspecting for behavior and tasks.
2) Set the team culture and expectation to do what is right versus what is comfortable to prevent regression to the comfort zone where failed organizations have died.
3) Create and maintain your freshwater tank for freshwater fish to sustain innovation through policy waivers and new policies to support pivotal initiatives.
4) Use technology and simplified workflows to eliminate the routine, technical, and mundane to empower teams to focus on high-order thinking and leadership.
5) Set the pace of change to hit the optimum opportunity window dictated by the external environment and pivot the organization as quickly as possible to avoid having to support competing cultures and systems.

ABOUT THE AUTHOR

E. Ted Fujimoto is president of Landmark Consulting Group that helps clients redesign their organization, scale innovations, and develop strategic alliances. Clients span across the education, entertainment, music, technology, and real estate sectors. In 1996, Ted cofounded and designed the Napa New Technology High School. The initial protocols used in the school to establish culture and for project-based learning originated from tools and practices used by his own teams. He then helped launch the organization that evolved to become the New Tech Network and helped Big Picture Learning develop its replication and scaling strategy. Follow Ted on Twitter at @tedfujimoto.

Chapter 3

AWAKENING: Recognizing the Context for Creating New Networks

If every day is an awakening, you will never grow old. You will just keep growing.

—Gail Sheehy

**CONNECTED EDUCATION VIGNETTE:
UNCLE RICHARD'S PLAN**

From analogue business cards to Twitter, what invites networking focus is finding the common points of interaction.

My own networking journey began in the analogue way; then in the late 1980s as mobile phones became more commonplace, I was very quick to adapt to purposefully writing my cell phone number on my business card as I gave it to a contact. This simple act showed a level of commitment to my contact at a time when mobile connecting was new.

It showed authenticity—that I was willing to be available anytime they needed me for any reason. My dad taught me very early on in our family small business that if you don't take care of the customer, someone else will. A key lesson for schools today is that if schools do not realize that students are our customers who deserve the best experience, students and their parents are going to leave public schools.

Education can change if school leaders recognize the need to change and have the willingness and commitment to change. When digital dots connected exchanging e-mail addresses in the 1980s, it actually meant that there was a certain level of trust gained. You could simply send a message via the "magic" of a computer. I used e-mail as a way to touch base and stay connected by sharing interesting articles or news, always aware of the fine line between sharing too much and not sharing enough.

Ahead of Facebook, I learned the art of sharing from an uncle, who was an insurance agent in my hometown of Shelbyville, Tennessee. My uncle Richard would always look at the newspaper on a daily basis and cut out stories and photographs of the townspeople highlighted, a scrapbook or a playbook. Little did I know that this simple act of connecting and sharing with people would one day be something that I modeled my own increasingly changing communication platforms around.

Today we are Uber connected. The challenge is still being seen as trusted and not just "how do we stay connected in a 24/7 world?" As an early adopter of technology, my curiosity was the driving force for me to join new social platforms. For me, Twitter was the place to be in regard to connecting with professional educational leaders. Educational leaders were quick to realize that they could create personal learning networks that would span the globe.

In my position as national director of strategic partnerships for Lifetouch, I had the opportunity to meet many incredible educational leaders through our partnerships with various national associations, such as the American Association of School Administrators, NAESP - National Association of Elementary School Principals, NASSP - National Association of Secondary School Principals, NSBA - National School Board Association, and PTA- Parent-Teacher Association. I enjoyed following them on Twitter. Just like the trading of business cards, following each other on Twitter was the new norm, a first step in continuing the building of digital relationships.

Contributed by Jeff Allen (@bjaj1)+35 year educational services provider, Gig Economy Specialist

It was never enough to just be a follower of an individual on Twitter. You need to be actively engaged, and that meant having conversations, not just retweeting other's tweets. I always tried to follow a ratio 80/20—80 percent being my original content and 20 percent of retweets. Another form of engagement was to engage in Twitter chats. I got over my fear as a noneducator of engaging in these conversations, and I soon found out how welcoming these groups were and how enjoyable it was to have an environment of cooperative learning.

The reality of having meaningful dialogue about common interest is the basis of my journey from business cards to Tweets and from uncle Richard to Twitter; "Relationships are always built and strengthened." New friendships, new connections, new partnerships, and, yes, new networks can begin with starting dialogue. Too often, we think networking requires some complex formula, but really, the process is simple and straightforward.

PIVOT TO NEW PRACTICE: "RECOGNIZING THE CONTEXT FOR CREATING NEW NETWORKS"

Many schools are places of rigid construct where systems are shackled to the status quo and innovation often seems impossible, but as the classic Bob Dylan song goes, *the times they are changing*. In spite of good intentions on the part of school district administration, traditional school models have negatively impacted modern student success in this rapidly changing, open, and transparent time. Many school organizations, newly awakened to a digital and tech world, recognize that they are isolated and siloed within dated, business-as-usual communication practices, and the relevance of a school district is becoming of importance and not taken for granted in a time of great transparency.

School superintendents, system leaders, principals, and teachers who still unconsciously follow the traditions of the idiomatic ivory tower, by working separately instead of collaborating, will miss reaching the desired result in a new age of student achievement. Using the same old systems isn't an option. In an accelerated time of change, this is risky behavior. Unfortunately, superintendents often see sourcing professional networks as overwhelming, as a burden, something else they have to do. They resist change. They miss the true purpose. Professional networks not only are an asset to the development of a school leader but also benefit students in tangible and intangible ways.

Building professional leadership networks is more than an add-on. It's practical and creative in nature and practice, and it can be a consistent part of a day-to-day leader's schedule. Professional networking is foundational in a modern superintendent's job description. These networks are viewed as something that leaders collaboratively engage in, not out of compliance but for empowerment, differentiation, and relevance. It's time for leaders to stop "living in their own algorithm," as the saying goes. Time to go beyond their safe and comfortable zone—to get connected. Thanks to online connectivity that we feature in chapter 7, you can see endless possibilities using social media tools for networking, connecting, and collaborating. There's no excuse for superintendents to operate in silos, remaining isolated in real time or online.

Today's high-paced, high-stakes, and highly connected changing world demands organizational performance and leadership effectiveness that is grounded in connectivity with stakeholders. These stakeholders experience this energy and exchange in most of their daily engagements. They want it in their schools. This is the age of the "PIVOT," and agile connected leaders are powered to new levels of efficiency. To start with one example, school superintendents, like Dr. Rob Zywicki @robertrzywicki on Instagram, who leads the Weehawken, New Jersey, district, knows the value of networking. Rob's ability to strategically use platforms and channels to communicate in digital and social spaces distinguishes his school, one that is recognized by its consistent Model School status, awarded by the International Council of Leadership Excellence.

Dr. Zywicki knows student success depends on the leader's ability to cultivate a connected, not static, internal culture of professionals trusted to create and maintain a new order of "business as unusual" in the organization to prepare graduates for a new world of work. It means breaking down barriers to learning and gathering partnerships that benefit kids.

At the root of organizations—even as the new machine age of AR (augmented reality) and VR (virtual reality) begins to scale—is a truth: *to communicate is human.* And communication is most efficient in organizations when humans work together for a common cause and do what they do best: collaborate and learn together for sustained growth.

Superintendents of vision see that professional networks are organic. They can be engaged in through an almost unconscious practice at the level of neural biology that suggests automaticity. Superintendents who are agile stop overthinking the call to networking, connecting, and collaborating. They just do it! On a subconscious level, overthinking is a construct that we build out of fear and doubt. It prevents discovery of new opportunities such as new networking partnerships that make a school more competitive.

When networking is embraced, the superintendency and overall organization reach new efficacy in communication power. Think about Google, Apple, KPMG, and other organizations that rely on networking to grow talent, market products, and reach new customers. System leaders in education are now called to follow the same formula as leaders at those global organizations.

Networking builds new thinking reflected in that business-as-unusual culture for your own superintendency. When Sir Richard Branson, one of the world's premiere business leaders, shared the short video of a whale exchanging hellos with a human, the Internet was delighted, but be reminded that the human sound made by the whale is a duplication of tone with no warmth, understanding, empathy, or hope for connection. The hello exchanged every day in a school is filled with these connecting human powers.

Leaders who promote the benefit of humans experience the synchronicity of networking. Collaboration that results positively impacts the behavioral waters of the very communities they lead. Networking without warmth, passion, and feeling is just another automatic, surface interaction in any given day filled with hellos and goodbyes. Adding warmth, passion, and feeling brings critical ingredients that can supercharge daily interaction and lead to possibilities of sustained longevity with partners.

Keep in mind that to network is to be human. Explore that fact through Bryan Kramer's H2H (human-to-human) model, one he proposed in 2014 to business leaders. School superintendents, like Branson, a chief executive officer of a multimillion-dollar organization, have a lot at stake in this rapidly changing communication environment for humans. We can't afford to simply hold our places in time. We are challenged to keep up with change as well as to exceed expectations.

Our responsibility to navigate this wild ride in a modern age of leading creates new conversations that address the importance of becoming collaborative in networked organizations. Districts where superintendents take the lead in cultivating a culture of relationship behavior, are districts that have a collaborative organizational culture.

School superintendents can be champions of collaborative organizational practice leaning into the spirit of teamwork, creating a culture of collaboration driven by relational behavior. When this culture of "becoming" blooms, student achievement is sparked. School districts cannot succeed without student success. Too often, school leaders, teachers, and staff members view district and school success absent student success. Students' interests come first and are amplified in networked school communities.

When superintendents become the connector, the chief leaders of "dot-to-dot," they model risk-taking that challenges the organization to rally and lead in their own unique way. Being collaborative advances learning and innovating existing against the grain of a hurried technological pace. However, this fast-paced rate can benefit students through an urgency, a just-in-time intervention and call to "do whatever it takes" for students to succeed on their way to the new world of work.

In this context, in our modern transparent environment where traditional school organization life is challenged, the relational side of an educational leader's career path can change the typical administrative day into something more distinguished, more human. Becoming relational is not a typical practice of school leaders, but it can become a remarkable part of their professional development. Creating a culture based on relational networks transforms an organization and makes the difference in the workplace readiness of any graduate of a school possessing this culture. Students are transformed from the experience of learning how to learn in a relational environment. These collaborative schools are places where communally understanding solutions, not just finding one answer, is valued.

Seth Godin, today's premier business marketer and author of 17 best-selling books on business marketing and organizational leadership, speaks of the conundrum of tech-challenged leaders in a socially networked world that brings fear of change. Many leaders fear the point of breaking away into a socially networked world. Godin, in his 2014 unique leadership book, *What to Do When It's Your Turn (and It's Always Your Turn)*, counsels leaders to be fearless communicators, speaking and publishing, inspiring listeners with "out-of-the-box" examples and strategies for creating new connected culture. As you start your journey to being connected, take heed of Seth's words and his vast collection of work, especially his content online and in print. His counsel is found in his daily "Seth's Blog," super-quick read that can quickly "upschool" your marketing self and add resource for school leaders who are anxious about the openness of networking.

To begin with Seth's word in mind, start "stretching." Here's a few practical stretching opportunities for superintendents for launching a more connective positioning:

- Join local community organizations, such as the local economic development board, chamber of commerce, hospital board, and civic organizations.
- Volunteer to be part of committees at the local, state, and national levels—look for opportunities to collaborate with other leaders, never limiting yourself to just educational leaders.
- Attend events outside of the educational arenas to expand organizational knowledge and diverse understanding of "new" trends in leadership that provides new opportunities for new partnerships.

Starting with simple deeds, open acts, and a model of connectivity, a leader can provide what a complex organization needs to begin the shift to being relational. Informed by a relational district leader, school leaders, teachers, and staff members can create successful, human-centered, networked, collaborative places where a focus on teamwork creates cultural pillars to support internal and external networks that pump energy and purpose into a static community.

Superintendents who create opportunities where all members of the organization have a chance to participate, network, and collaborate are on the right path to improved culture. Carving out time to network is not enough. Dictating cooperative behavior won't result in networking behavior. Step up. You are creating a system. Think strategically. Make collaboration and networking a systemic part of the superintendent's job function. Make it a tangible part of your promise to your school. This plan is the professional path to your career, post–ivory tower.

Today's open and transparent times contrast with the classic business-as-usual pace of many schools. Educational thought leader David Price explains in his book *OPEN: How We'll Work, Live and Learn in the Future* that if a time-traveler from the 19th century were beamed into our world, he'd be bewildered anywhere in the landscape—except in most schools. This thinking alone is a powerful reason for change. Districts today must shift from this business-as-usual isolation to collaboration, from going it alone to networking for empowerment. Taking on reform in the area of relational network development has its proven reward. Transformational leaders are more likely to engage in networks that will result in overall organizational effectiveness (McCreery, Mazur, and Rothenberg, 2011).

OPERATIONAL ALIGNMENT: CALIBRATING THE EXPERIENCE

Build a Networking Muscle

The best networks are more than a list of personal or professional connections. To calibrate their use to success, persistent practice in identifying and sustaining trusted connections is required. Superior superintendents recognize and activate strategically sourced relationships, internally and externally. This is essential to the health of a 21st-century school. Connected superintendents, acting as the CEO of complex and dynamic learning organizations, ensure that the district is not isolated internally, compartmentalized in its systems in the microenvironment, or distanced from the outside, the macroenvironment of the larger world.

Leaders reach externally seeking essential collaboration with public and private entities and internal stakeholders for student success. Reagans and Zuckerman (2001) suggest indirectly that today's professional and organizational networks are characterized effectively by four key qualities: (1) quantity, (2) relationships, (3) diversity, and (4) quality. Build your networking muscle around these ideas by strategizing which of these topics is a strength for you and which is a weakness in your current context.

Find your sweet spot of relational strength first. Then find the gap, the opportunity, in your connectivity. Connected superintendents will be able to determine if they have a high-quality network if positive, unexpected events occur because of their focus on connectivity. Your ongoing conversation with yourself as a lead networker will be about weaving those four traits into your strategy. Ultimately, success is determined by the leader's realization and embrace of continual learning and improvement and a willingness to change as organizational trends change. Networking is ongoing, and it is never a one-and-done activity. When you think you've nailed it, think again.

The creation of networks isn't a confined effort. It launches a culture that attracts change across an organization. Who can predict the serendipity of positivity that can follow in a networking culture that is adaptable, expansive, and amplified? Nobody. Anything is possible! Opening the door to networking culture will require work. Challenge may present itself due to the ongoing and changing demands on educational leaders. It is tough to be an "edge dwelling leader," because school climate has been traditionally built from the safe center—not the edge, but it is worth every effort. Calibrate yourself to build a dedicated networking muscle. As Seth Godin said, "stretch," start small, stretch yourself, go beyond, and connect.

Another hurdle for some is a unique issue of singularity. There may be only one school superintendent who shoulders the burdens and leads not only the school district but also the greater school community. Seifert and Bar-Tal (2017) note that educators operate alone, solo performers in schools and school districts. A distinct isolation is found in a superintendency. There may be several doctors, lawyers, and small business owners in a community but only one school superintendent.

In rural communities, the isolation is more significant. School superintendents who lead in remote, rural districts and are restricted geographically may find it difficult to engage with other educational leaders and community leaders, but we now live in changing times with tools that can make the gaps shrink in daily keyboard strokes. No excuses. Establishing networks refreshes a superintendent who can see beyond the boundaries of space and time to learn the satisfaction of connecting with other educational leaders—in a neighboring school district or a school district in another state—or even in offices where leaders work who touch your community.

Think big and work in small steps as you build a collaborative spirit that starts with your internal school community and expands outward. With the vision of moving out to external networks beyond the district's constructs, a spirit of new opportunity awaits in an age of connecting. The effectiveness of the superintendency and district is only limited by the status quo, which in the past has encouraged seclusion and isolation. Today, seclusion and isolation are two key drivers of inefficiency and ultimate organizational failure.

PAUSING FOR TECHNOLOGY: PRACTICAL ADVICE

Shake It Off!

Why should it matter that you get involved with digital and social becoming as you stretch yourself as a networking professional? It's the 21st century. What we do now to build networks couldn't have been imagined 10 years ago. The opportunities to connect are boundless. Recognize that you have a responsibility as a superintendent to own a strategy for building relationships that can be designed through a balanced strategy employing traditional and new age tools. As Michelle Carville cautions all leaders in the 21st century in her 2018 book, *Get Social: Social Media Strategies & Tactics for Leaders*, things have changed in the past 10 years, no doubt. "The objective is to know what you are doing on social media and, importantly, why you are doing it."

Know that face-to-face connection is a valued part of any new network you build, but turn your attention to the world online to connect. You'll be happy to know that the very same skills you bring to building networks online are the skills you use offline, sometimes called "real-time" relationships. It doesn't matter if you are shy or outgoing in your style. Trust, authenticity, curiosity, listening, affirming, and confirming skills are all a part of building analogue or offline networks. In chapter 5, you will find guidance for your personal brand

and brand management and learn how it fits into your balanced strategy for networking. In chapter 7, you will find a richly informative tool kit from educator and professional development consultant Judith Wilson, showing the social and digital values of the most popular social and digital sources presented using three questions: *What is it? What does it mean? Why should I care?*

The tools of a connected leader in the 21st century are skills that adapt from real time to online networking. Shake off the feeling of feeling overwhelmed. You can keep up with connections using a plan of outreach. Don't welcome the world! Focus on using a connective goal to form the foundational number of people you want to have in your system. For example, keeping a "Fast 50" contacts of networking "go-tos"—a list of people you want to keep close—use the image of a digital rolodex to "see" your community—has power.

Others act exponentially by simply asking trusted contacts online and offline. For instance, asking "who do you know that I should know?" as you attempt to build connections with trusted contacts who will offer you introductions is a great strategy if done sincerely and not in a first meeting. In addition, you can maintain new relationships with the help of technology by setting reminders and forming groups so that you keep checking for new contacts, even sending a short hello or a great article from a file of good leadership, management, or education or business pieces.

That gets you started as a trusted content curator for your network. When you have a Fast 50, help them learn. Give the gift of learning through a quick read of an article; send them value through free ideas. Tech tools are key to unlocking these new opportunities to present yourself as a trusted and authentic leader. Geographic borders, boundaries, and obstacles are no longer viable excuses. Tech tools allow for connecting, networking, and collaborating 24 hours a day, 7 days a week, and 365 days a year. Twitter, LinkedIn, Facebook, Voxer, and so on never sleep.

When you start, "listen in" on a platform by simply showing up on social Media daily or weekly professional conversation or "chat" and lean into finding interesting contacts and creating a group of those you want to strategically invite to connect online on the sites you observe. Survey the options to add tech platforms and be a curious shopper!

Have you spent time aimlessly searching through Facebook school sites to see how the lead learning superintendent is present? Keep a focus. Choose the channel best suited to your goals of building a network and collaboration through the use of technology by showing up as an open, listening, and connecting personality, a leader who uses technology that suits your unique needs and skills in a way that respects your time and place.

As you look across the landscape of networking with tech tools, do a first pass and choose a goal for yourself; then find a matching tool. In considering tools for networking, you can think about the longtime respected leadership platform of LinkedIn. Are you optimized on LinkedIn? A vast majority of current, former, and aspiring superintendents are active on LinkedIn. The wealth of knowledge that exists on LinkedIn for superintendents is unmatched. If you are not connected to superintendents on LinkedIn, you are truly behind and flying blind—as each day, ideas, experiences, and stories of innovation are shared that are truly transformative, even the most seasoned superintendent. Get yourself a good photo and write a summary that shows your personal professional brand, one we will explore in chapter 5.

It's a place where many business CEOs can show their leadership thinking through presenting themselves as "members" of an industry tribe and a place to develop content. It's the "safest" way to start building an external network, since it has the most leeway of how much to post and the platform offers video and text options to begin to build your profile.

As you survey don't discount Twitter as it can be a great "listening in" tool for news and information related to education and other industries. Everyone is out there: retail, media, manufacturing, and health care! It can help you connect to external business partners through CEOs of brands. Choose the Twitter success of the CEO of T-Mobile, John Legere, to inspire you. Set up a profile and follow him, and "listen" in to see how his tweets build his brand personality and the personality of his company.

Search among his followers. Anyone who is following him could be a great addition to your "listening" network. Add them in and follow. Legere embodies a listening presence on Twitter and engages positively with employees on his site. How about the world of visuals? We know that by 2021 80 percent of what is shared on the Internet will be visual sharing of video. Be bold by thinking about the connecting power of images.

If your goal is to become part of a leadership "camera culture," a term used by the Madison Avenue agency sparks & honey, an Instagram account may be a light touch way of becoming connected though positioning your eye on the world, showing your school's accomplishments and promoting the school brand. There's a wealth of choice from YouTube to Reddit to Snapchat. The digital opportunities allow you to add the idea of being a "social" leader to your résumé as you build new connections for your school! Networked leaders build and maintain connection through digital and social media presence.

Using technology empowers you because of its proven audience or stakeholder-facing power. No more ivory tower. You have a responsibility to build what is called a "digital footprint" as a leader. Start by googling yourself today to see what type of digital footprint you already have! Your community, those internally in your school and externally in your audience outside of the school, is transforming and growing too because of the pace of communication.

Add the emerging technologies of AI (artificial intelligence), VR, and AR that are present in the internal and external connected communities we serve. According to industry specialist and lecturer, Scott Kerr, @scott_kerr, of

Silvertone Consulting, AI has become a force "making everything that was old new (personal communication, April 18, 2018)." Conversation will now emerge as important, but it will interface with technology as speakers, assistants, and platforms intersect with our lives. These tech changes will impact your communication as a superintendent. You are looking at a tech world that brings business as unusual to our schools every day. Shake off the feeling of falling behind. Jump in. Embrace the network for today's and tomorrow's growth. Embrace the opportunity to do something great for students, by discovering the power of connectivity in terms of people-to-people connectivity!

SETTING A PACE: LEADING AS SUPERINTENDENT

Awareness. Purpose. Communication.

Something to remember about networks, according to thought leader Ted Fujimoto, is that some things never change and everything has changed. The human desire to gather and relate is part of our DNA. Human behavior has always been collectively positioned and oriented to working in a trusted group. That hasn't changed in our history. What has changed, and the fear that may accompany it for some leaders, is the way these relationships are now made and advanced in new social and digital channels. The idea of timing and pacing has never been more important in an Uber-connected world. School districts can change more quickly than imagined if powered by an informed networking culture and strategy.

This change is measured and balanced, not chaotic, sporadic, or rushed. Necessary collaboration doesn't occur overnight. If it were easy for organizations to change, there wouldn't be the wealth of content available to leaders on how to make it happen! Walt Disney modeled overcoming the impossible. He made the impossible seem fun. Yet, through overcoming the impossible he created enjoyment for millions and so many generations. Begin with hope and confidence. Superintendents set the pace of deliberative change in the district regarding relational culture. Again, change must occur but not a pace that leaves stakeholders breathless, which is detrimental to the long-term practice of cultivating a culture of collaboration.

We contend that superintendents should have a very clear, concise, and easy-to-follow plan to setting the pace for their pivot from siloed practice to open, transparent, and meaningful collaborating and networked practice. Like the business leaders who use the tenets of neuroscience to understand organizational behavior, school leaders can balance thinking fast and thinking slow, knowing when to claim the moment to connect and when to patiently build relationships. The plan to create this is found in three simple steps.

Step 1 in setting the pace for change is found in *AWARENESS*, the ability to recognize that change is needed. Too often, school districts operate under the false notion that perpetuates a comfort zone of business as usual: the status quo. This is your time to lead from the front and model. Though we are well into the 21st century, organizations struggle with accepting that problems exist and change is needed.

The isolation of superintendents in metaphoric silos, administering behind the closed doors and controlling decision-making, is still business as usual in many places. This view is seen by many in the rank and file as the best way to run an organization, large or small. Like business and enterprise is discovering, school districts must transform and recognize that change is critical and essential to launching a new strategy for step 1 in setting the pace and planning for networking evolution.

Superintendents or school system leaders will encounter times when decisions related to personnel and litigation and other decisions of confidentiality may have to be made behind closed doors, but these are moments of respected focus that are reflective and deep that should be the exception, not the norm for decision-making style. Organizations that are shackled to the status quo are destined to fail—history is crystal clear.

Complacency and acceptance of operating from the rigid constructs of the past leads to customer disengagement, brand blandness, and loss of market share—remember BlackBerry! The same is true with school districts. When school districts fail to change, students become disengaged, learning becomes stagnant, and competition from other learning organizations overtake the local community.

In establishing *PURPOSE* in step 2, a leader purposefully determines the school system's capacity to change and to create a culture of collaboration. Before pivoting to a new order can happen, before networking can occur, the leader takes the temperature for change and studies the future: does the school system, collectively, have the capacity to change through my leadership efforts? Do individuals have the ability to create change or network knowing there is a model in the mind-set of the leader to change the status quo?

Change processes can be big or small, but at either level, the people creating change have the will and tools to carry out the change process. In very simplistic terms, the capacity to change requires, according to Creasman, Bacon, and Franklin (2018), a vision, an understanding that change is a journey and not a destination, buy-in of stakeholders, the empowerment of others to be leaders (change agents), the determination to create change, follow-through, and looking into the future for how the change can be improved.

These principles of transformation that Creasman, Bacon, and Franklin provide are key steps that can be used to create a culture of collaboration and set the pace. Utilizing their principles of transformation as the lens, step 2 can best be accomplished by leaders in search of collaborative change using a series of guiding questions that lead to a pivoting toward networking culture. To prepare for the pivot, leaders self-assess and then seek feedback from trusted partners using the following questions:

1) What is the district's vision for change and collaboration?
2) What resources and supports are in place to encourage change and collaboration?
3) How are stakeholders encouraged to be involved in the change and to collaborate?
4) How are stakeholders empowered to be change agents and to form new opportunities of collaboration, internally and externally?
5) What are the district's principles for change? Are collaboration/networking valued?
6) How are leaders and other stakeholders provided professional learning opportunities that encourage change, help individuals to acquire and develop the skills, and, more importantly, provide the confidence to collaborate?
7) How will the change process and the push to create a culture of collaboration occur? What will the change look like?
8) What happens when the change process is executed and a culture of collaboration is created? What is the plan for tomorrow?

Superintendents who wish to create change in their school districts and a culture of collaboration use these guiding questions to establish the right pace for their district. The key is to keep focused, a hand on the pulse of the district and speed up and slow down, as needed when it comes to networking, collaborating, and changing a culture. Speeding through change only leads to overlooking critical components of the change process, stakeholder confusion and disengagement, and ultimately failure for change to happen.

Step 3 is *COMMUNICATION*: communicating to your stakeholders specifically why the district must collaborate and network. Communicating the expectations for collaboration and networking as the model of these processes assists school superintendents in engaging and empowering others to leave their cubicles, offices, and other silos that have formed. A few communication guiding questions follow:

- How will collaboration lead to student success?
- How will collaboration lead to more effective and transparent decision-making?
- How will collaboration lead to improved district operations?
- How will collaboration improve the district's capacity to lead?

Start with explaining why collaboration and networking are important to the school district and also student success. Holding an initial brainstorming session or early adopter conversation about this change gets you out there, seeing around corners at new possibilities. Explain with a few simple reasons and examples how collaborating and networking can help each individual grow in his or her position and make the roles more interconnected with other roles in the organization.

Talk to the people you work with to get real examples about the power of collaborating in their personal and professional lives, and have them "testify" to this power. In the past, allowing silos to form communicated, in essence, collaboration and networking were not needed in schools. Today, collaboration is not optional but a necessary part of the school district's long-term strategy. The topic can be addressed in casual and formal settings, which is why it has power.

A critical communication strategy is to keep communication regular. Continue to have dialogue in the district about the importance of collaboration. Regular communication helps keep empowerment high and on everyone's radar but also at the forefront of all decision-making. Stakeholders need to be repeatedly reminded of the focus, the vision, and the importance of collaboration by the superintendent to keep it fun, engaging, and expanding!

SPOTLIGHTING BUSINESS ACUMEN: PRIVATE SECTOR APPLICATION

Be "Human2Human" in Today's Connected World.

—Ying Zhou, Program Director at Tech Incubator at Queens College

When Trish Rubin talks about the H2H model, it strikes a chord with me. No matter what we do, we are all humans. Networking is nothing but making a human-to-human connection. As humans, we each have our own ideas, thoughts, knowledge, and access to resources. It is in the exchange of our human experience that each of us grows. George Bernard Shaw once said: "If you have an apple and I have an apple and we exchange these apples then you and I will still each have one apple. But if you have an idea and I have an idea and we exchange these ideas, then each of us will have two ideas." Networking allows us to have more and more ideas and to grow more connections.

When I first started in the business world, networking used to mean an exchange of business cards. Nowadays, I use the H2H model. Networking for me means to make a human-to-human exchange as a connection, to learn something about the other person, to learn something that I did not previously know, to figure out what I can do for the other person, and to explore mutually beneficial collaboration opportunities.

Networking is a deliberate practice of making a human-to-human connection. It can happen anywhere and not just in business. It can happen at a bus stop, in the hallway, at an event, in a workshop or a conference, on LinkedIn or Facebook. In fact, if we replace the word "networking" with Bryan Kramer's term "H2H" and live that every single day, connectivity never fails. I invite you to give it a try.

Today's superintendents must be able and willing to network with other leaders and other external stakeholders. Superintendents face the stress of public education challenges: mounting pressure to address the achievement gap, stagnant budgets, a growing teacher shortage, new forms of high-stakes testing, and a diversifying student population. The pressures that superintendents face might encourage them to retreat to their offices; however, now is the time for superintendents to reach out, collaborate with other leaders, and establish networks and partnerships that will lead to removing barriers to effectively leading today's school district and lessen the pressure.

Herminia Ibarra, is a professor of organizational behavior and the Cora Chaired Professor of Leadership and Learning at Insead. She suggests that "Networking is vital for successful managers" (Networking is Vital for Successful Managers, 2007). Leaders are encouraged to network. Ibarra says that in today's interconnected world, leaders rise and fall based on their ability to network. Those leaders who network are more likely to be successful, while those who choose to remain isolated and shackled to their internal constructs are likely to fail. Read Ibarra's full article by scanning the following QR code.

PIVOTING POINTERS FOR CHAPTER 3

- Be willing to reach and stretch. Recognize that standing still and remaining isolated is not only career ending but actually detrimental to the organization—the school district.
- Collaboration and networking must be a tool in every superintendent's leadership toolbox.
- A networking "digital footprint" matters, which can be balanced with your offline networking efforts. Start to explore the various ways to build networks through tech, and begin to educate yourself into the right fit as a leader.
- Recognize the opportunities that collaboration and networking provide school superintendents and their staffs, and, more importantly, what a connected school culture offers students in their paths to becoming college, career, and life ready. Collaborating and networking, at the end of the day, are about creating the best experiences and opportunities that will provide a high-quality education to every student.
- Focus on *AWARENESS* for building networks and why this is essential for your success in today's quickly changing world of communication.
- Understand your *PURPOSE* as a school superintendent and the purpose of collaborating and networking in transforming an organization that overall has not changed in 50 years, a school district. Highly connected superintendents, through creating a culture of collaboration within their districts, bend constructs that impede change, organizational efficiency, and student success.
- Key in on *COMMUNICATING* from the start. Find like-minded, early adopters who have a love of collaboration to help you build your initial steps into a new persona of networked school leader.

Chapter 4

BECOMING: Innovating and Disrupting beyond the Traditional Ivory Tower

Leadership and learning are indispensable to each other.

—John F. Kennedy

CONNECTED EDUCATION VIGNETTE: AN UNFORTUNATE SITUATION, A POWERFUL OPPORTUNITY

Dr. Katrina Applegate, superintendent of Winchester ISD No. 1, a small district in the upper Pacific Northwest, was going into the fourth year of her first superintendency. Dr. Applegate had experienced prior success. Student achievement increased, and student enrollment was up, but as the fourth year started, the legislators in her state made severe budget cuts. Though budget cuts were a common thing that many school districts had to face, Dr. Applegate had been fortunate enough not to have experienced the challenge of cuts.

A former high school principal and assistant superintendent for curriculum and instruction, she began her first superintendency in a small district with a small tax base, where the majority of education funding came from the state; raising taxes was not an option for Dr. Applegate as she attempted to protect learning programs from deep cuts. She quickly learned how to stretch every dollar for students.

Over those four years, Dr. Applegate was reluctant to attend the local co-op for superintendents made up of 10 local school districts from small and large school districts, both male and female with varying years of experience. The co-op meets monthly for lunch and an afternoon that consists of legislative and educational updates but more importantly sharing out strategies and seeking help from the group. Suddenly, Dr. Applegate was faced with trying to figure out how to protect her school district from cuts and continue their success. She decided to attend the next several co-op meetings with other superintendents.

The networking experience was positive for Dr. Applegate, her school district, and other superintendents. Not only was she able to learn strategies of how to overcome budget cuts, but she also shared with her colleagues her experience with personalized learning in a small district, for which the state had recently recognized her as a *next-generation superintendent for innovative technology practices*. She was able to utilize the local co-op of superintendents to establish a critical partnership that helped her to gain valuable learning and led to her district's continued success without suffering significant cuts due to a reduction in school funding.

Dr. Applegate used an already-established leadership network, the local cooperative of superintendents for her professional growth and the growth of the district. This network of local superintendents was available at no cost to her or the district and resulted in many positives. Though the cooperative met only once a month, the relationships Dr. Applegate formed with other superintendents allowed for her to call them anytime that she had questions. The same was true for them as they ventured into the arena of personalized learning in their districts. Though engaging in a professional network was out of necessity for her and her school district, Dr. Applegate embraced the opportunity to form lasting partnerships that continue to extend into the classroom and help her students and teachers succeed.

THE NETWORKED PRINCIPLE OF BECOMING: PIVOT TO NEW PRACTICE

Becoming Innovative and Disruptive Beyond the Ivory Tower

We all recognize this famous movie quote from the *Star Wars* films, "May the Force Be with You." Spoken positively it's a rallying cry for battling dark forces; the underlying concepts of this charge to a community resonate with leaders. CEOs of Fortune 500 companies often speak of disruptive forces within their organizations, internal and external. Disruption is a part of organizational life and is not necessarily a bad thing when necessary change results. Not being prepared for disruption can be damaging to the company's long-term strategy, brand, and overall bottom line. Just ask Kodak—or Blockbuster, which once had 9,000 stores worldwide and now has one store left in the United States, about the need for preparedness!

The past 25 years has seen the most dynamic surge in human learning and capacity building ever seen before, and the networked world can be thanked for that fact. Educators are part of that surge. Disruption is creating a new future. School leaders are investigating an edupreneur stance!

The timing is perfect for an innovative model to emerge, according to Jason Renshaw, general manager of Learning, Culture and Capability at Australian Unity, "Innovation is about creating intersections between different domains to see what emerges on the other side." Add the professional learning power of sophisticated networking skill to an innovative spirit, and superintendents have a leadership toolbox to keep pace with the changing world.

Today's school districts need to be urgently disrupted, as the organizational model for most school districts in the United States has changed little over the past half century. As author David Price reminds us, most students are still taught in rows with a teacher at the front of the classroom lecturing for 60 minutes or more. In 2018, the majority of students are still taught like this, which continues to plague America's global readiness and competitiveness. Why?

The students in these classrooms already represent a highly connected networking community through their personal social networking behavior. They are already innovating as digital natives as their school leadership remains shackled to the past lacking in innovation, collaboration, and creativity. The result is organizational isolation. Silos still remain in school districts. This organizational model must be disrupted quickly if the American public school system is to prepare students for employment in a connected world. Too many students endure an outdated learning model that discourages inspiration, discovery, and collaboration. Networking is a learning organism, and it exists in the state of mind of becoming. Its role in a school, although seemingly disruptive at the start, is an engine for connected school change.

School superintendents, like CEOs of Fortune 500 companies, strive to recognize that there are beneficial internal and external forces that demand a culture of collaboration and strategic networking. Internal forces are those forces at work within the organization. These forces are subtly present in the causally connected networks but not recognized as a systemic part of a communicative, collaborative school vision.

In our school community, these loosely maintained networks consist of kids, teachers, staff, and parents. These groups have clout and influencers. These influencers can be useful to the school organization. External forces impact the organization from the outside. Environment, politics, economics, and technology all play a part of influencing school collaboration and relationship building and networking.

The key for superintendents is to learn to utilize both the internal and external conditions to ignite a collaborative and highly networked culture throughout the school district, one that is always in a state of becoming something more, something better, and engaged. If school superintendents accept that positive change can occur from disruption to the status quo and embrace the internal and external "business-as-unusual" view of networks, they can confidently lead people to accept an always-becoming mind-set that keeps the school system agile and not static.

Superintendents are the "gatekeepers" in school districts of the daily administrative routine as well as the long-term vision for the organization. They have to have their finger on the pulse of the moment and their eye on the prize of the future. Because of that stance, superintendents can act as the gatekeepers of collaboration in a longitudinal view, encouraging not preventing collaboration.

School districts are slow to adapt to the new and typically resistant to change because of the limiting constructs that have developed overtime. Janice Bruce, a New York City school principal, is attempting to change her leadership narrative. She has experienced a limiting construct of leadership that she calls "it's all your fault." She wants to combat the business-as-usual default to blaming the principal.

Janice believes that change is not impossible with the brand message that defends your professional image and promise. She is in the zone for building her continual learning and becoming. This can start with your recognition of the power of collaboration through professional networking efforts. A construct that plagues many of the school districts across the United States is isolation, yet most employees in culture surveys indicate the desire to break away from its grip and collaborate and network.

This desire to collaborate is a force that when unleashed can change the organization's culture and cause a ripple effect throughout the district. A disruptive stance, the targeted leadership of networking in support of the already loosely established internal connections, creates needed communication innovation.

The Pixar Company is an example for superintendents to use as they study how to build collaboration. Pixar prides itself on collaboration as a means to encourage creativity and innovation. Its headquarters is characterized by spaces of creativity and collaboration. Isolated decision-making is not even considered—among a team of the world's best creative artists. Pixar emphasizes the motto, "another digital work created by the TEAM at Pixar." They work together, collaborate, and enjoy the awards as a team. The key takeaway for superintendents is to create spaces that push back on the forces of isolation and give way to forces of collaboration.

The Pixar culture can be part of school culture. Just connecting with the idea of a more modern, open workplace is a possibility for introducing collaboration. A compelling example of Pixar culture is found in the disruption of the typical notion of classroom space, leading with a simple question, "what would a learning space of today look like?"

One forward-thinking superintendent, Dr. Shari Camhi, Baldwin, New York, has acted with laser focus over four years bringing new classroom models from the workplace into her school settings. A disruptive move that has been lauded by her community and beyond, it's a future-forward concept that her internal community saw along with her, bought into with commitment, and that has led to amazing external connections.

Dr. Shari Camhi reached to external partners, Google and Mashable, for help in visioning the new learning spaces. She honored her internal system, asking her custodial staff to partner in the design and build out for 47—and counting—classroom renovations created at the insistence of her teachers who bought in and lined up for the change! That system not only kept cost to a minimum but also gave the custodians a "becoming" experience, allowing them to use their creative construction talent to make each individual teacher's unique, flexible learning environment!

In the process, Shari connected to the Omni channel opportunities to tell her story of the school's vision, getting media and press partners to showcase the collaborative efforts to audiences outside of the school walls—all in support of preparing her students for working and learning the jobs of the future. "Education usually doesn't readily accept what's different," Dr. Camhi suggests that *education usually doesn't readily accept what's different,* but that doesn't stop this superintendent. By linking the project with the school's core value, tangible and remarkable evidence of 21st-century education resulted. Pixar, take notice!

Other experience supports the stories of connected leadership and the power of stepping out of the comfort zone of your familiar school setting to meet the challenge and joy of finding the journey of becoming a way to solve problems as the story of superintendents Michael Lubelfeld and Nick Polyak shows.

> As new superintendents, we had to access networks to lead organizations that were growing and on the verge of transitioning from a rigid organization into a student-centered organization. We both had the convenience of our location to be able to access a variety of networks; most were educational networks; however, some were not. What we learned was it didn't matter what network we participated in, we walked away with a plethora of information, resources, strategies, and in fact, more contacts.
>
> Each time we networked, we met new leaders, people, strategic connections that have helped both of us improve our effectiveness as leaders and educators, and become better collaborators. It has been our experience that teachers, principals, and superintendents limit themselves by confining our experiences to classrooms and schools. In today's high-stakes culture, we need to expand our connections and seek new opportunities to experience, grow and collaborate. There is nothing wrong with educators and educational leaders expanding our networks, as there is a "buffet of opportunities" that offer education field

valuable lessons and experiences that can be used to create student-centered school districts.

—Michael Lubelfeld and Nick Polyak

There are many bright forces in play in school districts, which can be recognized. As addressed in chapter 1, one of the strongest forces is collaboration. To network is to be human. Presenting the positives of creating a new way of charging your organization, breaking out of just settling for the status quo, and going past being risk averse to wanting to make gains for a school through networking are bold parts of your strategy.

Humans being humans will be risk averse, unless leaders are communicating on a daily basis with verbal and written support in favor of network building, and with commentary about growing and becoming connectors. Leaders communicating clear benefits of networking to their communities through collaboration show the way.

Through moments of face-to-face discussion, chats, informal focus groups around a cup of coffee, there will always be that elephant in the room of "why should I care about networks?" Make your first campaign to be one of modeling benefit through stories, content, and examples from districts that have chosen that caring road. Take a quick look at James P. Grieve School of the Peel District School system, district in Ontario, Canada. Its Twitter feed proves this point. The school district promotes itself as "the place where the best dreams happen when you're awake!"

Connected school leaders model and participate in collaborative behavior with their staff. Connected school leaders loathe the word "I," as it signals that you win through isolation. Instead, communicate successes and failures in terms of "we," which says as a team, they will win together.

To create and encourage collaboration in your school district, try these simple strategies:

1) Create an open environment of becoming. This means that superintendents, district leaders, and staff are always open to new ideas, while encouraging creativity and innovation. Furthermore, the office has open accessibility. Doors are always open, which encourages colleagues to visit each other, collaborate, and make shared decisions.
2) Be transparent. The kryptonite to collaboration is restricting information. Decisions must be made out in the open, and information, with only legal restrictions, must be freely accessible to everyone. Transparency creates a sense of collegiately and a team culture.
3) Focus on trust. No team, whether an organizational or professional sports team, is going anywhere if trust is missing. If school superintendents expect collaboration to be a pillar throughout the district, trust is the key.

OPERATIONAL ALIGNMENT: CALIBRATING THE EXPERIENCE

Relational Leadership

Think of your own internal organization. Most employees want to be affiliated with something. They want to belong. In chapter 6 we will show more internal network opportunities for you to cultivate. Belonging, which we will highlight in chapter 8, a big part of the culture of networking, is reinforced when people gather around common causes that are relevant to them. The stories that are shared from finding others who are "Like Me" are the first emotional hooks to accepting the power of networking.

There is nothing more powerful in an organization than a superintendent, one who strategically steps out to gather people around a shared disruptive idea or vision. A leader who celebrates this behavior and the activity surrounding it does so strategically, not on a "one-off" celebration based on a calendar but an infusion of communication of collaboration and networking into every part of the organization life of a school community.

This leader is in a continual state of becoming. The world today, according to Kevin Kelly in his 2016 book *The Inevitable*, is in that same state of becoming due to the intense rate of change. Welcome this stance as a way to invite collaboration. Release people from fear of trying something new.

A leader who guides people through collaboration fights isolation in favor of becoming and sees adopting new communication commitment to networking as a disruptive practice. The 21st-century school leader who pushes school superintendents to reach across normal boundaries and form strategic partnerships, friendships, and collegiality with other school superintendents, business, and community leaders to grow the district in myriad ways is the epitome of a disruptive leader.

Opportunities to be disruptive exist anywhere the superintendent leads. According to the Organization of Economic Co-operation and Development (2003), there are a variety of networks to be accessed, diverse in the field of education. The superintendency, by position and status, brings with it the possibilities for unique opportunities and the potential to create a school system that is solely about the success of all students. By tapping into collaborative networks, success is amplified.

Leading today's school districts, no matter the size, location, or type, is no easy feat. Each day brings new challenges, new opportunities, new situations, and new pressures to succeed. Coupled with a true darkness of a Star Wars–like value, the underlying force to remain the same persists. The "dark side," which is powerfully negative in school districts, is a primary reason why the tenure of a superintendent is only three to five years.

The dark side is those forces that push for isolation—rigid constructs—which kills innovation and creativity and compounds fears of risk-taking and job security by working in teams. Superintendents to overcome these powerful and negative forces must focus on the positives. They must communicate why a team approach to decision-making is better than making decisions in a vacuum or behind closed doors. Furthermore, show how job performance, which means job security, is improved through collaboration.

Superintendents can again think in a balance, identifying a few select "new" disruptive behaviors with recognized ways. Model the pace of taking on new disruptive leadership stances knowing networks take time to grow. Creating a district that focuses collaboratively on the success of *all* students is no easy task. Get started and build connections that can get you to the level of responsiveness that helping all students. Fear of bringing the new to the now and getting disruptive as a networked leader will hold the district back from becoming an organization that is student-centered, teacher-engaged, and parent and community-supported.

Many superintendents use geographic or positional isolation as an excuse to not engage in collaborative networks. This is simply an excuse for becoming more connected, and its resistance impacts other leadership or organizational factors. Leadership networks are more than just connections between friends and business contacts; they are powerful points in a universe that many leaders simply fail to understand or recognize. Each point, partnership, offers school leaders access to powerful opportunities to share, acquire information, and confess their concerns and mistakes.

Leaders, in the past, resolved that their positions were naturally isolated, never questioning the constructs that restricted the leadership position. Superintendents who want to choose a disruptive communication stance through networking begin to challenge the idea that leadership must be isolated in order to be effective. This belief not only is inaccurate but effectively contradicts the research and understanding that leadership is strengthened through empowerment of others.

Today's successful school organizations are about empowerment, instead of control. Leadership networks built to disrupt the status quo help leaders fight against being stuck. They spark transformation, not only for the superintendency but also for the organizational structures in schools. Ted Fujimoto counsels that we must create and maintain a freshwater tank for freshwater fish to sustain the disruption and innovation through new policies to support pivotal initiatives like building a connected networked culture, so the initiative is sustained.

The superintendency has many available networks at its fingertips, a literal buffet of opportunity. Progressive superintendents now form collaborative external partnerships with neighboring district superintendents, vendors, and even local elected community leaders. As the story at the start of the chapter illustrates, a consistent, trusting community of like-minded superintendents can resource each other. The positive spin of being the school CEO, "Chief EVERYTHING Officer," is well placed in networking. There is limitless possibility of everything good in building your CEO stance as you collaborate and connect.

Superintendents often dismiss opportunities if they appear to be different or cloaked in different fabrics of success and possibility. There is a beauty in the way your own network can be tailored through attention to a collaborative collective. Building a professional leadership network isn't a one-size-fits-all proposition. Too many organizations, like school districts, operate based on arbitrary constructs, generic and cookie-cutter principles that lead to only stagnant growth and performance.

To standardize what a professional leadership network is is to limit the options and opportunities for strategic growth, collaboration, and partnerships. Superintendents must stop trying to rationalize everything through a dated lens from a time when collaboration was seen as weakness and empowerment was a step toward mutiny. Superintendents can recognize that the opportunities that exist to form new disruptive connections can result in highly impactful professional friendships.

School superintendents taking on a business-as-unusual and even disruptive approach to leading can act within the IKEA effect, a metaphor for building something you need yourself! Here are a few ways to do this quickly in IKEA style:

- You need a network, so *get going* and *learn* as much through search, google, interviewing, and listening to get solid with valuing a disruptive notion of being a relational networked leader.
- *Audit* the networking behavior in your community through management by walking around, which can help you find the networks that are already in place in your school community.
- *Recognize* the potential of professional leadership networks. If opportunities do not exist for you to engage in collaboration with other educational, business, or community leaders, keep the IKEA effect in mind; be willing to forge to paths to these powerful partnerships.
- *Create* opportunities through strategic moments of "assistance." Leaders who want to network need to be open to listening and be tuned to recognize the opportunities when someone is in need of assistance or has a question. In business, leaders utilize the chance when someone asks a question or needs help to not only garner a sell but also market their product and obtain information. They also use the opportunity to form collaborative friendships and partnerships that can lead to an expanded professional network.

- In addition to *calibrating yourself* through assistance, *recognize* that superintendents are typically seen as the chief education expert in the district and community. When in pursuit of information, strategies, and resources that will help to improve their school district, see this as an active time for listening and acting to build new relationships. Don't fear saying "I don't know," and replace the phrase with "I can get that for you."

These opportunities can lead to an excellent way for the superintendent to form networks with critical individuals and stakeholders in and outside of the community, who are in the know of the things that they don't know. Take advantage of curious behavior when you are asked to provide assistance. When anyone from a community member to a state legislator asks a question, take on the can-do attitude of a curious learner and ask questions in an e-mail, a phone call, or even a well-crafted tweet. Calibrating in this way helps you become connected quickly to potential networks that are powerful, you seeing yourself in a bit of a disruptive light—as chief executive officer of the school district.

When identifying a long-term strategy, start your processes going, not with an "ask" but with a value proposition. Use a first e-mail, LinkedIn request, text, or phone call. Tell your story about building your innovative and disruptive effort within your organization and through the digital platforms of the external world and in your real-time moments. The work to establish these connected systems of collaboration quickly subsides as superintendents, along with other leaders, begin to grow their roles as leaders.

Networks beget networks. Organizations are changing, resulting in new forms of networks developing within. The organization is being recreated, restructured, and expanded based on the individuals within the organization and their new internal and external networks (Hickman, 1998). They are always in a state of becoming. It's a contagion that spreads when people truly collaborate, not from ego but from the heart. Look around, and see the potential. A one-time experience within the organism of networking may result in long-term partnerships. Though the opportunities to network may not be readily available to start, you make them happen.

PAUSING FOR TECHNOLOGY: PRACTICAL ADVICE

Embracing Change and Nudging Relationships

Today, school superintendents have a variety of digital tools that can help them "disrupt the status quo" and make connections unheard of even five years ago. Still, we can take advantage of the earliest types of disruptive marketplace thinking as we balance our professional leadership network in real time and online. We don't have to be aggressive or heavy handed with adopting a new digital presence. We can embrace change by nudging our communities through building an awareness of our commitment to changing culture through patiently building a networking presence.

Consider this back in "the day" attitude. Once upon a time in business, people created powerful "hot dog on the street corner" opportunities. Business or organizational leaders never waited around until opportunities presented themselves, and they have always gone out to create opportunities for success. If business leaders need to sell hot dogs, what do they do? They go out, find a street corner, and start selling.

Each street corner brings new clients, new opportunities to form new relationships with clients and future networks. They know that engaging with the audience, showing up, is a big percentage of making an effort successful. They get out there and nudge! Can we adopt that street corner attitude to our digital connectivity as we learn to network online? We can embrace that in our early efforts.

Invitations to network at events, meetings, and conferences are occasions that are not going to come in the e-mail each day. Superintendents, especially in those remote areas, can create the nudge toward networking online in their own time and at their own pace. Awaiting to be summoned to the table is a losing strategy, especially in a time of such access. The fact is that most people get news, keep up with friends, get directions, get questions answered, shop, and make doctor's appointments and reservations on mobile phones. With clever platforms like Calendly, the digital appointment driver, you don't need an assistant to schedule your quick connections to that Fast 50. Schedule 15 minutes and keep connected!

This should be a proactive indicator that any superintendent with Wi-Fi access is already personally "out there" and can think about showing up on any digital "street corner" and start getting professionally engaged. Opportunities to establish new networks are literally in the palm of your hand. Worldwide ownership of mobile phones with cellular connections is about 7 BILLION owners.

No one can use the "distancing" argument as a superintendent. You must show up on the street corner with your mobile for the most immediate interaction or, if you must, on your laptop or even desktop computer! Just like the owner of the hot dog stand, superintendents need to make the rounds in educational networks and noneducational networks to diversify their network. Superintendents must recognize that there are only so many superintendents in the nation and teachers, but many more noneducational professionals and leaders who are already sharing ideas and content that form the basis of collaboration.

When superintendents think about taking a small step into the position to nudge their network, they can imagine the good feeling that comes, first from the internal community, when a more active digital presence on the part of a leader is observed. From the first efforts, this projects a new sense of openness and transparency toward the superintendent, which creates the beginning of new relationships of trust within the community.

Many leaders of big companies such as Goldman Sachs have caught the attention of employees by acting disruptively on digital platforms as they opened up their profiles on social media. What's powering them is the digital footprint mentioned in chapter 3. It's a footprint worth investing in, but make a plan as you do. Again, change is occurring all around school districts. Now is the time for superintendents to jump on the bandwagon and encourage district-wide transformation. Take a wrecking ball to those antiquated, outdated, and negative constructs that are plaguing the organization and preventing innovation, creativity, and collaboration. Here's a way to create a framework that will elevate your innovative stance.

- Start by making notation of all the people you may want to connect with as a digital networker. Separate the list into three categories: (1) PEER, (2) ASPIRATIONAL, and (3) REACH.
- Start making a list of the "Like Me" people who are your PEERS, who are "like you" in whatever capacity that means.
- Then make a list of those whom you aspire "to be like"—ASPIRATIONAL contacts, including those you know and those you don't know.
- Finally make a list of the REACH people who are far from you in terms of likeness, but they have an interest value about them—something that may connect you eventually and turn them into "Like Me"! These are the people with whom you want to associate.

In the book *BrandED* by Sheninger and Rubin (2017), there is a developed reference to help you choose those with whom you want to associate. It's called an ACE strategy, and we will explore it with tools in chapter 8. It is a bit of marketing strategy that you as a business-as-unusual leader will need. Like any good marketing communicator, use a bit of segmentation, a sorting of the community according to common persona and features. This activity will help you approach the digital networking landscape once you have chosen the platform you want to use. It's so important to know why you want to be on any digital platform and to know the real value it can bring you as you network, so be deliberate in deciding whose attention you want to get.

Once you have your list ready, do a quick search of the most important in your framework. You can use your laptop in this process to give you all access to some of the features of platforms so that you see a good profile of the people you want to know. Make note of what common features you may have with each of them. This is often referred to as "responsible stalking"!

You are taking time to understand the persona of a potential member of your professional learning community. People who are not just educators but those from far-flung industries and interests want to be part of the respectable stalking you develop.

As you set out to build this network, face the voice in your head that may caution you on taking time up to do this. *Ignore that voice.* Focus as successful consultant Ted Rubin, @tedrubin on Instagram, does. He promotes networking ROR (*return on relationship*), which comes from forecasting what value you bring and what value will be returned to you by sourcing new connections. Again, once you decide which platform you want to focus on in digital, your methods will be tailored to understand the *return on investment* of time and the ROR of being on any platform.

Don't forget digital. You create the power. Create what marketers call "omnichannel" opportunities. If you are in a school district that is limited in leadership contacts or geographically isolated, a digital presence can help you create your own opportunities to engage partners by telling the story of your school. Use a *Field of Dreams* strategy, "If you build it they will come." And once they are there, keep them engaged with your responses, your content, your authentic short online musings, and presence!

SETTING A PACE: LEADING AS SUPERINTENDENT

Strategize. Belong. Engage.

Forming a professional leadership network is doable with a strategy and a balance of real-time and online goals and objectives. The saying "Birds of the same feather flock together" is an excellent metaphor for starting your first venture into leadership networks. That fits the "Like Me" strategic list you will build. In most cases, leaders attend events with other leaders or talk daily with other leaders in their same field. Leaders use these daily occurrences to establish reliable networks that will only strengthen over time.

As you move into calibrating your behavior as a networking leader, be assured that these consistent touches will create what marketers call "stickiness" in your relationships. Networks exist to provide opportunities for professional development and colleagueship, and position purpose and efficacy (Lieberman and McLaughlin, 1992). Be conscious of your effort.

At this point, a superintendent might be wondering about engaging in a pace that simultaneously includes both an internal and external network. Based on experience, countless interviews, and familiarity with networks, we would recommend that superintendents access networks that best align with their needs and organizational capacity. As mentioned previously, superintendents should access internal networks first as a way of initiating their new behavior, coming out of their comfort zone.

An internal network can be the testing ground for developing trust, core values, and brand as we will learn later. But since this is a unique process to every leader, nothing says the superintendent can't engage in both at the same time. Internal networks are between leaders and staff members, while external networks are made up of internal staff and external staff members.

There is also an opportunity for superintendents to access multiorganizational networks where they engage in growing their networks with the help of new relationships in the internal network that offer reach into networks that may include noneducational leaders who share a common goal or interest of the school community. Superintendents may want to start with accessing their sources in the list of their "Like Me" peer network as they venture out to make external connections.

Superintendents who aren't invested in the local professional organizations for superintendents miss an excellent "Like Me" opportunity to connect with other superintendents and school executives. Each state has superintendent associations that are partners with AASA, The School Superintendents Association, the national association for superintendents, and provide limitless opportunities for superintendents to connect at the national level in a variety of programs such as the National Superintendent Certification Program, the Urban Superintendent's Academy, and the Women's leadership Network.

The AASA provides a program that matches each superintendent's need. According to Davidson and Middleton (2010), associations often provide the only organized forms of networks for individuals. Nevertheless, many superintendents fail to recognize that programs, like the programs offered at AASA and other organizations, provide valuable personal and professional networking opportunities that can lead to growth.

Recognizably, AASA is the largest network of superintendents in the country; it is not the only organization that offers networking opportunities. The opportunities are just as numerous and diverse as the superintendency is. Many organizations cater to the large city and district superintendents, small and rural superintendents, female superintendents, and minority superintendents. Embrace each opportunity that these organizations offer, and pace your engagement with new targets that create positive disruptions that yield new relationships, not random, superficial connections.

SPOTLIGHTING BUSINESS ACUMEN: PRIVATE SECTOR APPLICATION

Be out there and be Involved!

—Jeffrey Kraft, Senior Business Development Officer, Investors Bank

I first discovered the power of networking in college. Although very reluctant at first, I used my father's connections to get me an interview for a summer job at a NYC bank. Well, I got the job. I was asked back the following summer and then joined the bank's management associate program after graduation. Not being too proud to use a referral (whether a parent or a friend) is an advice that I continue to pass on to others. It is often not what you know but whom you know. My first networks were really developed in high school and then college. Without really knowing it, my love for the game of tennis allowed me to meet many people whom I stay in touch with for essentially my entire life.

My advice to other professionals is simply "be out there and be involved." I am active in the Rotary. I am on four not-for-profit boards and not just as a member but rather as an officer/leader. Find time to take the lead. You can also create your own groups by looking for a common thread, such as providers to professional firms or business owners or dads with daughters. Usher at church. Organize a block party. Be involved in community service projects.

Far from my strength. LinkedIn has been useful. However, nothing beats making a phone call or dropping by to have coffee with your clients, prospects, and friends.

I learned some valuable tips from a few senior executives in the banking world. Tom Sayles (former CEO of Summit Trust Company) taught me the value of remembering names, using them when seeing people—and knowing at least one personal thing about everyone.

Later, I found out that Tom kept a drawer filled with index cards and business cards where he had notes about everyone he met—then, just before seeing these people, he would refresh his memory! To this day, I have done the same. Insofar as a sales guru, I have learned a lot from researching and reading about Jeff Gitomer. Some of my own advice: bring your own name tag to events, one that is easily read, and wear it on the right side. It is a handshake thing. ALWAYS carry business cards.

Arrive early to events to meet the host(s) and to "help greet" the other guests as they arrive. An hour and fifteen minutes is usually plenty of time to accomplish your goals for being there. Know who is coming to dinner—by that I mean get a list of who else is expected and do your homework on them. Follow up with everyone you met within 24 hours—no exceptions—after that they have forgotten you. The result is in the follow-up. Their connection, their "gifting," will distinguish you from the pack. Send a newspaper article, recommend a new restaurant or book, and so on.

Do not keep score. Be a giver first and second. When someone hands you a business card, look at it and make a comment or ask a question; do not just stuff it in your pocket or purse. The person is proud of what he or she just gave you. Today I serve as mentor to new Rotary members and look to help my younger colleagues in business.

When you attend events, bring a guest in another field (with permission from the host). Step out of your comfort zone and participate. Arrange your own roundtable discussions with 8–10 people from different disciplines. Get three new contacts/names every time you have a meeting with someone. Be a speaker, or offer to get one for an organization that overlaps with your interests. These practices have worked for me, and I am glad to share them with fellow professionals.

Adding to Mr. Kraft's strategies, recognize that there is a buffet of opportunities each day for leaders to network. According to J. Kelly Hoey (2017), for most, the word "networking" only leads to feelings of discomfort. But the pain that most leaders feel is the result of a misunderstanding of what "networking" is. Networking is so much more than having cocktails and making small talk. In Hoey's (2017) *Forbes* magazine article, learn about the "Five Networking Opportunities Hidden in Your Average Workday."

PIVOTING POINTERS FOR CHAPTER 4

- Professional leadership networks, though leaders may be familiar with the term, have always existed as collaborative webs of reference and support.
- No matter where you are in your superintendency or where you are located, engaging in professional leadership networks now has a balance of real-time and online strategy to "nudge."
- Collaborating doesn't necessarily have to look big, bold, and sexy. Superintendents should look for existing opportunities to collaborate and use new strategies to leverage their reach—don't discount local organizations, co-ops, and civic clubs.
- Too often school superintendents say they do not have time to network—they have students who need to learn. But networking does not take some elaborate and time-consuming process. Superintendents can have a robust network with other superintendents who may be close by or long distance by literally picking up the phone.
- A studied approach to focusing on forecasting your robust network starts with segmenting a digital audience into three segments.

- Building a professional learning network is not a one-size-fits-all proposition. Leaders find themselves engaged in an IKEA effect, building their network on their own and pacing accordingly.
- Starting with a plan that addresses making connections internally and leads to external connections may feel the most comfortable pace, but knowing the networking is as individual as your own fingerprint can lead you thoughtfully to develop both networks at your own pace.

Chapter 5

BRANDING: Owning the Image, Promise and Result of a Leadership Networking Brand

> Unless you have absolute clarity of what your brand stands for Everything else is irrelevant.
>
> —Mark Baines, Global CMO Kellogg Company

CONNECTED EDUCATION VIGNETTE: THE POWER OF PARTNERSHIPS

Dr. Bill Allen is a new superintendent of a large school district in the upper Midwest. He follows a 20-year tenure of a retiring superintendent who had been in the district for his entire educational career. Over the past four years, this superintendent experienced declining student achievement, increased absenteeism, and increased teacher turnover. On hiring Dr. Allen, the local school board challenged him to transform the school district over the course of his first four-year contract.

Dr. Allen's career provided him with valuable learning experiences. He was a teacher, principal, district director, and most recently assistant superintendent. He was ready to jump in but quickly realized that the district lacked a valuable asset, external partners. Over his career, Dr. Allen transformed a school and helped a district to transform through partnerships with other districts, colleges, and local businesses and community organizations. He was surprised by the fact that his new district, due to its size, had not formed strategic partnerships.

While investigating the lack of official partners, he came to realize what had discouraged partnerships and collaboration: the district had developed a brand in the community as an organization that did not want to partner with local businesses or community organizations. Dr. Allen discovered that this predecessor had refused to form partnerships with the local community college and university on the basis of personal reasons from the past.

The local businesses, community organizations, and even other surrounding districts saw the district as arrogant, only reaching out when it needed money. The notion that the district takes on the personality of the superintendent was validated by what Dr. Allen discovered. The school district's brand had become the brand of the former superintendent who pushed back on any form of collaboration, favored running the district from behind the desk, and saw partners as individuals who wanted something for themselves, not for the district.

The former superintendent had not spoken to neighboring school superintendents in years. Dr. Allen, a leader who favors collaboration, understood that turning a district of approximately 55,000 students around to a positive view was not going to happen overnight, and the job was only made more difficult without existing supportive partners. Fortunately, Dr. Allen's brand as a leader is well established among colleagues.

In simple terms, his brand was recognized as *"a transformative leader who valued collaboration, valued feedback and input, and worked to engage and empower ALL stakeholders in the organization."* As assistant superintendent, he worked with other assistant superintendents in the region to show his brand, forming a partnership to create a virtual learning school for at-risk students so that they could graduate with a high school diploma.

The students, Dr. Allen, and other assistant superintendents were all focused on the risks. Many students were one step away from dropping out. Some of them had already dropped out once due to the school's constructs that were not conducive to their needs or learning interests. The regional virtual learning program helped reduce the dropout rate in the partnering school districts by almost 8 percent over the first three years. Dr. Allen attributes the virtual learning program's success due to the partnerships and not anything he did as an individual.

Dr. Allen knew that if he was going to turn around the district as the superintendent, he had to work with others to change the district's brand quickly. He stressed to others in the district that change does not happen through the work of one individual but an army of change agents working together for one common purpose. Dr. Allen knew that if the district continued to work as a "siloed" organization in the community and region, it would never be successful and continue to see the same results: declining student achievement, increased absenteeism, and teacher turnover. He worked to re-brand the district as an organization that had transformed and was now ready to partner with the community and neighboring districts to create learning opportunities that would result in better outcomes for students.

Today's superintendents must recognize that their organizations that they lead have a brand, whether positive or negative. Branding is more than just a slogan, vision, or motto published on letterhead. Branding is strategic down to the size of the logo on t-shirts, brochures, and websites. Look at Independence Community School District's Communications and Marketing Guidelines at http://www.independence.k12.ia.us/district-information/communication-guidelines/. They convey the importance of their brand down to the millimeters. Brand detailing and strategic networks established through a robust branding plan are needed in schools today. If this is news to you, then chapter 3 is precisely what you need to read as you prepare to network.

We would also encourage you to read Dorie Clark's article, "Why Public Schools Are Finally Getting Savvy about Marketing." Clark says there is too much at stake for school leaders not to develop strategic marketing plans that are used to sell their school district's brand. But she encourages school leaders to go beyond just developing a marketing plan, but also have a strategic communication plan that will be used to market the district's brand. Read Clark's full article in *Forbes* magazine by scanning the following QR code.

THE NETWORKED LEADERSHIP PRINCIPLE OF BRANDING: PIVOT TO NEW PRACTICE

Brand Image and Promise That Create Result

Engagement expectation has come to schools. Our communities are steeped in daily engagement through the 24/7 news cycle and mobile access in all areas of life. This sets the expectation of parental access to the experience of sending children to school and the expectation of response from those who provide the experience. The internal structures of a school, sometimes referred to as the microenvironment of the school experience, are now tuned to digital and social access to two-way engaged digital communication and the demand for personalization that is expected.

The third-party and crowd-sourced communication that comes from social media engages the external environment that touches schools; the larger macroenvironment surrounds and brings engagement in complex, fast-paced ways. Be excited by this state of affairs! It is exciting to know that the micro- and macroenvironments can offer countless opportunities to build a culture of networking, a vision of connected performance by those in the community, and the promise of partnerships that come from a networking strategy. The opportunities that exist today, unlike five years ago, are remarkable and transformative.

Before you get your virtual handshake on and get your networking ducks in order to engage, consider an essential step that precedes a leader's launch of a networking plan. BRAND! Create a leadership brand *image*, make a brand *promise*, and commit to tangible *result*. Develop your own leadership story and share it. Doing so is not self-serving promotion as your brand will power the school brand. Having a professional leadership brand helps leaders to pivot to a connected leadership stance. Today "edu-brand" is essential. In short, know who you are and what your brand core value is before you network—take time to build a brand that will empower you in this "age of expectation." Show that your care about your brand and that it matters to you before you journey to "making friends and influencing people," as Dale Carnegie suggested in his groundbreaking work on collaboration.

Having your own story of your "unique brand value" (UBV) opens the door to networks, partnerships, referrals, and friendships. Superintendents who recognize the importance of establishing a positive, leadership UBV elevate the activity of networking and raise their chances of building multiple connections. According to Schawbel (2010), actively engaging in networking can improve an understanding of personal brand and also expand the professional network. This is the power of word of mouth—a well-developed and clearly communicated personal brand travels. There is a saying "Who you are is how you lead." Therefore, start thinking about your UBV. The same can be said about "who you are is how you connect." That brand you create will attract those who have shared attributes in their own UBV.

School leaders must approach professional leadership networks as an opportunity to form connections that will enhance the district's brand. Yes, that's true—but start on the personal professional level with yourself. Before working on your school brand, which can be part of enlisting the internal network of your school, before you lead a district effort, you must experience the brand-building experience in a highly personal way. Superintendents' brand will be the "calling card" for district connectivity.

A superintendent's brand must be consistent and aligned with his or her network(s). Both brand and professional networks are interconnected, and the success or failure of one means the success or failure of the other. Professional leadership networks often lead to school superintendents to evolving their brand as a means to remain relevant and to expand connections in aspirational ways. The core of a superintendent's brand is solid, but the promise may evolve as a network becomes more diverse.

Adding some psychology to the mix assures your understanding of how that brand can be advanced. Social and organizational psychology confirms that authentic leadership brands aren't ego driven, so be authentic! Branding and networking are essential to the superintendency. The best networkers embody the philosophy that it is better to give than to receive.

Wharton School professor Adam Grant's book *Give and Take: Why Helping Others Drives Our Success* (2014) attests to that fact as well. Today's highly effective superintendents are leaders who empower others internally in the school organization and externally in the macroenvironment, by giving support and resources to succeed—one result may be the collaborative creation of school brand. A modern school's chief executive officer must know that the superintendent's brand is about definition.

According to Yong Zhao, professor and author, *"Define before being defined"* should be a superintendent's call to brand action on a professional level. Get on the road to networking with a well-defined superintendent brand, one defined by collaboration, empowerment, strategic thinking, and leadership. Knowing that you already have a brand and understanding the critical value a positive brand holds are two essential first steps in branding for networking and developing a leadership brand that spreads throughout the district's organizational structures.

OPERATIONAL ALIGNMENT: CALIBRATING EXPERIENCE

Be the Storyteller-in-Chief of Your Networking Plan

Superintendents must recognize that with every new connection they make using a well-defined brand, they amplify their own UBV and eventually the district's brand. Because of that fact, the need for a superintendent to be what educators Sheninger and Rubin call in their book *BrandED*, "The Storyteller-in-Chief," is evident. Having an educator leadership brand is a necessity in a transparent world. The word has spread about leading through a narrative, and according to Paul J. Le Blank, president of Southern New Hampshire University, *"Leadership is about being Storyteller-in-Chief, crafting a vision and a narrative that inspires people to embrace the mission, gives them a sense of meaning, and impels them to do all they can in service to the mission. This is true of leadership at every level."*

You must be perceived as your authentic self online and offline. Avail yourself of the tools branding has to create to connect you to your authentic identity. It is important to take visibility to heart in this transparent time and move toward a person brand, not into self-promotion but to a higher visibility of communication that allows you to make your ideas, your presence, and your work more tangible so that you can lead your teams better as you reach to find external partners for your school. The superintendent's brand strength and district's brand strength will be told in an ongoing narrative to benefit students.

Stories that spread through the energy of "word of mouth" and stories that illustrate the educator's brand value will attract others who want to form partnerships and will strengthen and grow the educator's brand. It is a give-and-take relationship as your brand connects with others whom you want to align with for the good of your school. You will be able to garner influence with potential partners as never before. Influence is king in a digital and social age!

A negative leadership or organizational brand prevents access to more positive brands and limits networking opportunity. Today, public education is regarded in a mixed view at best and in a negative brand light at worst. A growing number of parents, community members, and especially legislative leaders at the state and national levels have lost faith in the system—and the school brand. Certainly, in many places, there is no developed brand to be seen. Making connections may be hard at the start in schools with negative perception. But it's not impossible with a brand plan to change this situation.

Over the past two decades we have seen a rapid increase in students attending charter schools, private schools, and home schools. Leaders can launch their own brands and build networks where they tell a clear story, as the storyteller-in-chief, to mitigate against loss of student bodies and funding. Superintendents have the chance to collectively re-brand public education, but first they must brand their superintendencies. As servant leaders in public education, we can benefit by adapting a model that's been successfully used to build trust in the marketplace.

In their book *BrandED*, Sheninger and Rubin took the lead in articulating what educator brand is, what it means as it is adapted to schools, and why it matters to public schools. An easy way to establish connection to brand power and to behavior and culture is through your own eyes as a consumer. (Remember reaching for coffee: which brand are you loyal to when you do?) Do you want to be a model of UBV for superintendents? You need to add a bit of marketing strategy to your *ConnectED Leaders* Networking Plan. Focus on what educators often miss out of a sense of humility and a fear of seeming self-promoting. We miss out on focusing on leadership selves. Get past being humble. You are telling your story of connection to your school to benefit that school and your students. Students, staff, parents, and the community need to have a leadership brand that they can connect with today. It's time to shine, school leader, and to recognize the promotional value your own brand currency brings to the betterment of your school community.

As you set about pivoting to a defined personal professional brand, calibrate by understanding what brand is about. In its definition, brand is seen as the sum of experience people have with a product or service. As a servant leader, the superintendent is out there every day serving up a brand experience and delivering an educational service. As you dig in to find your own brand, lay a foundation for becoming the storyteller-in-chief for your school. Start by thinking: what is my school district's brand? Does your school have one beyond a mascot? What is the core value of the school? We would encourage superintendents to start by asking this question to students as they are the most important customers in the educational business. The answers you get can help you see the urgency of crafting brand in your organization.

The first consideration as you build your own brand is the same thinking you will use as you lead a school brand effort. Build your brand the school brand using a simple formula. Do as marketers do; they attend to *image*—what is perceived a core value—and articulate the messages around that image to stakeholders and potential partners. It is the cornerstone of your brand. This isn't an elevator speech. It is meaningful and binding. Then understand that every brand has to define a *promise*—an offer that is short, easy to understand, and connecting. Take it from a brand that is taking on eBay that calls itself "the biggest marketplace you never heard of." The brand is "Tophatter." Have a look at this platform to see a UBV. The promise COO Andrew Blachman lives every day is "we spark moments of fun and fulfillment." Your school promise can be that engaging.

Revisiting an example of promise cited in the 2017 *BrandED* text, leaders can be reminded of the promise LeBron James made to the city of Cleveland, one he delivered on a promise by bringing a professional championship banner to the city of Cleveland. At present, we see an evolution in a promise to his hometown. We see his dedication to promise in the education space with his foundation's "I Promise" School launch. Keep in mind that we don't need superstar benefactors to build a brand. We do need promises that everyone keeps. Brandi Davis, longtime Akron educator and now the principal of I Promise School, makes her very public offer:

> To be more than just a traditional school principal, to tie in a social-emotional curriculum, to bring in wraparound supports for the families, and just to have an open and welcoming communal atmosphere.

Those goals can be shared by most schools and delivered authentically out of any school's school brand promise.

School leaders who can get tailored and tight in their brand promise don't need an elevator speech. They need communicating an original value that "sticks" with people about who they are that is unique to them. A brand image, maybe even captured in ONE word, and an offer, as you go out to connect, is your promise? Asking yourself what your district would miss about you if you weren't there can get you closer to crafting an image and promise in your personal brand reflection. Finally, challenge yourself to show *result*. Let's face it: what gets measured matters. Therefore, how will you tangibly hold yourself to acting out of your brand? Thinking back to Duckworth's strategy gives you a basis for measuring how your brand is measured for impact. Thinking of *image*, *promise*, and *result* can quickly help you into a mind-set for growth as a branded networker.

A school superintendent with an expansive view of networking presents a new possibility of brand awareness to the whole community. This leadership brand is one of inclusivity and allows superintendents to access a larger group of diverse networks. According to Kaufman, Vrontis, Czinkota, and Hadiono (2012), an organizational brand gives prospective connections, partners, and network symbols that reflect their own ideas, feelings, or experiences when associated with the organization.

The positives gained by networking using a clearly professional superintendent's brand and school district brand are limitless. School superintendents continue to face challenges. Network contacts can help their school partners close gaps, work past barriers, and overcome any obstacle that may confront the organization or leader personally. A trusted network of colleagues is what Regis Philbin would encourage contestants to access on *Who Wants to Be a Millionaire*? They would phone a friend when they needed help with a question in their pursuit to winning a million dollars.

In the recent case of previously mentioned Dr. Robert Zywicki, superintendent of Weehawken, New Jersey, a dramatic event occurred that interrupted that most sacred rite of passage, the senior prom. The happy ending to this story was provided by his external network! The entire network in his macroenvironment wanted to help make a memory for the class of 2018. Rob's network saved the event, and the students actually got a prom redox with the help of the connections in Dr. Zywicki's community. Bad press turned to good press overnight! Leaders, educational and noneducational, in the superintendent's network can help identify critical strategies and offer valuable supports and mentorships that often are not available elsewhere.

Your professional brand is exhibited in your role as a school superintendent daily. It is perception. The story you are telling in real time and online builds perception that you control. Building brand must be a serious undertaking for maintaining presence in this hyper-experience engaged world. School teachers, principals, staff members, parents, and the greater community recognize superintendents mainly by their deeds and actions, not necessarily by their title and name.

It is imperative for superintendents to own a visible brand, one that can serve as a foil for times when things go wrong. If you have a transparent trail of stories that you have told as the storyteller-in-chief, that record of your authentic brand allows you to confidently speak in tough times from that position you have taught your community into learning—your brand—and that authentic brand will rally all of your supportive, trusted networked partners; remember calling a friend on the TV program? Your trusted friends will step up for you and your authentic brand in times of challenge if you get out ahead of crisis and continually build a brand that they are proud to support.

As superintendents, the development of brand is critical to the creation of networks, connections, and partnerships that bring opportunity. Using image, promise, and result can lead you forward in your thinking. Leaders who are somewhat recluse restrict their network from being open and welcoming to others and other opportunities for collaboration with other networks. Leadership styles differ, but even introverted leaders can develop a brand based on their true selves as easily as more extroverted leaders do. Introverts work differently but still make connections as strong as those made by extroverts. Just tell your story!

Making sense of this new brand-aware behavior to others is part of calibrating for brand awareness. Spend many moments talking to your community about how you have built your brand and why it will be important to the networking effort you lead. Use a framework from the book *BrandED*, by Sheninger and Rubin, to show why brand matters. The term "CPR" (Culture, Performance, Resources) can connect to your brand efforts and networking efforts. You are breathing new life into the district through *"Brand CPR."*

Your brand storytelling efforts will positively charge *culture*, will expand stories of *performance*, and will result in new stories of connections to *resources*. When you open up those new channels for communicating—especially digital—your community will see evidence, the result of your brand engaging with the internal and external, the micro- and macrocommunity. New channels of communication, utilizing your network of colleagues, critical friends, and partners, will help solidify your brand as a leader and your organization's brand as a student-centered organization. In marketing, the term "signature storytelling" is a strategy of telling memorable, authentic stories that give leaders room to connect since they aren't argumentative or challenging in nature.

Superintendents can achieve branding success by being consistent, being specific, being true to their word, being true to themselves, being bold, and being authentic. These essential traits are perfect for superintendents as they begin to form networks and mold their leadership brands. The networks that are engaged with the leader's brand should be consistent with the leader's own brand, be precisely aligned, and be connected to the superintendent's ideas and beliefs.

These are varied networks that push the superintendent out of a comfort zone and spark courage in the superintendent to be creative and innovative, a person who thinks outside the box, and allow the superintendent to live in his or her authentic brand image. Superintendents who have a grasp of their own brand and are comfortable with their brand will not be afraid to take risks, stretch their own networks as they look to grow professionally.

PAUSING FOR TECHNOLOGY: PRACTICAL ADVICE

Becoming the Storyteller-in-Chief through H2H

In businessess, CEOs are now moving past old models of B2B (business-to-business) and B2C (business-to-consumer) and thinking about people through the model introduced in chapter 3 known as H2H. Business thought leader Bryan Kramer coined H2H ("human-to-human") networking in his 2014 book, *There Is No B2B or B2C: Human to Human: H2H*. The amazing part of that model is that you can take the same elements that have been advanced in the first chapter as a necessary part of a human skill set. Use them with people online as well as in real-time ventures. By doing so, you are using H2H. Research is supporting the balance of real-time and online networking. An H2H view can help you stay the course.

Keep yourself in balance as you use connective technology tools for building your brand. Don't err on the side of dismissing technology. Don't hide behind your technology to build a network. Keep both going as complementary ways to advance your brand. The process in both communication lanes starts with listening and understanding the goal behind introducing your own crafted personal professional brand into a network. Brand inspires your effort to be transparent and communication. But you have power over how you elect to share your content.

Think back to other times when you had to take on a new challenge, the first time you accessed a computer, got on the Internet, or sent an e-mail instead of a fax. These are challenges we all faced and now laugh about. The same can be said for getting up to digital and social speed as a networker. You can't be left behind today. Try innovating your behavior "inside the box" first in offline networking and then go outside the box to new lanes of digital platforms and social media that mirror a lane of face-to-face comfort.

For example, choose a goal of meeting like-minded superintendents in your region for a "TALL coffee," a SHORT on time and TALL on relationship building session. If you are concerned about topics to discuss, try a news feed app like Feedly, whose tagline is "Never stop Learning—Get Smarter!" Let the app gather content for you to learn and share with your growing network on your feet, on the phone, or on the screen through social platforms.

Choose content around marketing as you take on a brand perspective! When you meet outside of a school environment for coffee for one hour, you can hold a casual conversation powered by your search, or you can be more structured. For instance, at each meeting you rotate the responsibility to choose a challenge and focus on it in three ways. *What is the challenge? What does it mean in our day-to-day work? Why do we need to care about it?* Getting a tribe to unpack a common challenge is one way to make the challenge less daunting.

Now translate into further engagement through a digital newsletter or a Twitter chat; share a Google Doc or a GoToMeeting or Zoom meeting. Apps like WhatsApp, featured in the chapter on social media, chapter 7, also provide direction and help. But again, make time outside of your school environment for less distraction and concentrate on making the connection frictionless. Your goal is listening and sharing, which leads to resourcing your network. Think of adding a plus one—a new member to the group—after you've gotten comfortable so the tribe grows. See how that shapes the conversation and how the network increases along with your brand trust.

Another way to convene around the concept of sharing information can be through connecting to the edWeb online learning platform. Check out the schedule for live webinars, and meet online with your network to hear a topic that is a match for the network membership. Invite people in and connect through the online chat feature, or use a webinar that has been archived, and watch the session and follow with a real-time meeting. These are just two ways to see the balance of using the same H2H skills in person as you do online.

Should you want to give Instagram a try, check out chapter 7; set up an account and find other superintendents who are online. Ask your couthy peers or regional peers at meeting where they are placing their efforts. When you find them online, make sure to tag them with your posts around school and in the community. Ask a question in the post under the photo that gets your group to comment and to post their own photos. Simple lines of communication with colleagues can expand to rewarding experiences for superintendents, their faculty, and their students.

A way to start tracking your own digital brand footprint is through a googling search. But more opportunities lie in tracking key words about yourself, your district, or community through www.mention.com. LinkedIn can also be a useful tool for presenting your professional brand through a summary where you can capture your image, promise, and result as you look for others who share your attributes to grow your network.

Paying for the inmail upgrade on LinkedIn allows you access to approach aspirational networking partnerships. LinkedIn also offers a "social selling" score, which allows you to value your digital footprint as compared to the community online. Adding video to your LinkedIn platform from school or community can boost your score. Simply dedicating time every other day or daily to write a short line in your LinkedIn status about what you are doing to build your community that day will provide you with reach to others who are sharing key words and attributes.

Most importantly, identify only one or two channels to try out their benefit. As you grow into use, many of the platforms will introduce you to new features that keep you interested and connected. Remember when setting up your profiles. Keep consistent pictures, words, hashtags with other platforms to intensify the chances of the platforms power you to more users who will partner with you.

SETTING A PACE: LEADING AS SUPERINTENDENT

Visible. Emotional. Consistent.

The amount of pivoting and transformation that institutions must go through to come even close to delivering on statements of "preparing students for the 21st century" is sobering. The typical hierarchical decision-making depends too much on the limited abilities of even the most competent educational leaders to understand enough of the dimensions of how the world is changing to make well-informed decisions.

Networks and information garnered through them can help. So many of the largest stakeholders in education as well as regulators are barely comprehending the rate of acceleration and are unprepared for the level of change in society that is occurring. Professional leadership networks are the most important practice to all sustained organizational transformation; they help a leader cut to the core of what is important and prioritized and what resources are available. Networks help a leader's ability to pivot through the most critical moments in moving through disruption and innovation to transformation and sustenance.

Taking on brand as a serious leadership pivot is a commitment to identity and trust, to authenticity and collaboration. Brand efforts go far deeper than typical claims of excellence and preparation for the 21st century that schools fall back on as they present a face to the public. Settling for a typical description of your school is almost a "learned helplessness," to use the term that University of Pennsylvania professor Martin Seligman coined in regard to organizational change. People aren't hearing any difference in excellence. Today's stakeholders want to see illustrations of what that means. They want to "feel" the UBV in your school, as they do in the car they choose or the coffee they drink.

This status quo acceptance covered up with tired taglines that keep us locked in stock educator language phrases has long fallen on the deaf ears of an engaged community who wants to know more about our image, our promises, and our results. They want to visualize, to be excited, moved, and touched. To make the pivot into a brand that makes a network a powerful communication system, leaders must create the emotion that connects to people through their own personal brand. Social and emotional well-being in an organization, in a school community, is essential for well-being and acceptance of innovative new thinking, like the thinking that networks bring.

A major step in the pivot happens when a leader uses a business tool to build a brand called a SWOT analysis. Marketers use the categories of STRENGTHS/WEAKNESSES/OPPORTUNITIES/THREATS to honestly assess and audit themselves as they attempt to articulate a brand. In addition to strategies mentioned previously, a leader can sit quietly once or twice or as many times needed to reflect on the context. Where are you in facing each of these values?

Entering examples in each quadrant of these four descriptors helps to flesh out the story of leadership at that moment in time. Creating a SWOT and then writing a reflection into each quadrant deepens a leader's appreciation of the value of each segment to the goal before taking action. Sharing the SWOT with a trusted colleague or a member of any sort of established network can help confirm the self-reflection.

Having the SWOT on hand, creating a one-word descriptor, or using three power words to tell your story in real time and online can help distinguish you as you move forward to build networks that will welcome your presence.

SPOTLIGHTING BUSINESS ACUMEN: PRIVATE SECTOR APPLICATION

> Be a connector of people.
>
> —George Calderaro, University Community Relations
> and Communication Director
> Columbia University School of Professional Studies

I have spent my entire career in communication roles and therefore had the great opportunity to work across many departments within and outside my organization. As such, I discovered the value and rewards of reaching out and making connections for professional purposes as well as personal satisfaction. My work helped me become a connector of people and groups to knowledge and experiences, which I find endlessly rewarding.

It sounds simplistic, but the best way to develop networks is to attend as many events as possible across your field(s) of interest and to treat each of them as networking events. I am not suggesting hard-sell-all-smiles-and-a strong-handshake, but clearly any event you value will attract an affinity group which should be assessed and cultivated in a strategy. Technology allows almost anyone to be accessible or at least findable! As with all networks, relevance and affinities are the leading drivers for developing relationships. Take advantage of those that suit you.

Increasing my network, I usually turn to the "subject matter experts" in any given field, preferably ones with whom I am acquainted even tangentially and/or others who are when I need specific connections. I find that people are keenly interested in interacting with and learning from those outside their fields. If they know what's good for them, they will welcome fresh perspectives and/or new topics. Genuine interest from new contacts—as opposed to contrivances or superficial interest—should be enthusiastically welcomed and also flattering to potential new network contacts.

PIVOTING POINTERS FOR CHAPTER 5

- We live in the age of engagement and must accept the reality that our leadership skill set must offer our communities an open and transparent way to communicate and an authentic voice with whom to communicate.
- Brand development is a serious part of 21st-century leadership that precedes any strategy to build networks. Build a professional brand first as an imperative, not a choice.
- Leaders can reference the work of marketers and social scientists as they educate themselves about brand and as they create their own leadership brand to use is connection to professional networks.
- Every superintendent can craft a UBV to be used as a networking storyteller-in-chief.
- Brands are built through the understanding of image, promise, and result.
- To prepare communities to craft a school or district brand, a superintendent must process the experience as a leader and model the result.
- A branded connected leader uses the reason for this professional effort as a community "brand CPR" project to improve culture, performance, and result.
- Brand behavior in real-time networking and online networking is similar and related to human-to-human community.
- Leaders can adapt a marketing/brand tool called the SWOT to self-assess their professional brand development by reflecting using strengths/weaknesses/opportunities/threats.

Chapter 6

DEEPENING: Inspiring Internal Networks for Community Growth

Intentional development and participation in Professional Leadership Networks is a powerful proactive strategy to ensure all teams at all levels work together across the organization in an aligned manner. It becomes central to how one leads and vital to how the organization functions.

—Ted Fujimoto

CONNECTED EDUCATION VIGNETTE: "OPPORTUNITY TO LEARN AND PARTNER"

Russell Terry is a veteran superintendent in a large Midwestern school district. When Mr. Terry took over the superintendency, the district was experiencing a budget gap of approximately $15 million due to poor planning in recent years and continued decreasing student enrollment. Mr. Terry came from another state. He had experience with budget gaps and cuts, but nothing would have prepared him to address the $15 million budget gap he faced stepping into the role of superintendent. He had a lot of learning to do in a short time to meet budget time lines and prepare for the upcoming school year.

Mr. Terry called around to other neighboring school districts; however, no one could assist him with trying to close a $15 million budget gap as many of the nearby school districts had never dealt with cutting $700,000. He persisted. He learned the financial systems in the district and found someone who could help him in addressing this major budget issue.

After months, a superintendent in another large school district in his former state suggested that Mr. Terry and his team join ASBO (Association of School Business Officials) and begin the process of connecting with other school business officials online or face-to-face. Mr. Terry's contact suggested that he attend his state's ASBO convention to form partnerships with other superintendents but more specifically with school business officials in larger school districts.

Over the next several months, Mr. Terry grew friendships and partnerships with a variety of superintendents and school business officials in his state and across the nation. He was able to connect with a few school superintendents and business officials who had successful experience with closing budget gaps and also creating financial stability going forward. Mr. Terry's contact, a member of his network, in a different state, was a valuable asset, who helped connect Mr. Terry with an army of collaborators.

Mr. Terry was able to use the networks and partnerships he formed through ASBO to acquire the skills necessary to grow and to move the district forward. More importantly, he was able to show financial stability and communicated extensively regarding the district direction. Through the challenge, Mr. Terry grew professionally. He modeled his expectation of connectivity and openness and learned leadership lessons through building a network for collaboration.

THE NETWORKED PRINCIPLE OF DEEPENING: PIVOT TO NEW PRACTICE

Inspiring Internal Networks for Community Growth

A modern day superintendent understands that collaborating is no longer an option. It's a critical component of the job. Committing to collective organizational growth ensures the needed collaborative and distributive leadership stance essential in this digital age. As you approach this chapter, take stock of where you've been. You've taken on the role of storyteller-in-chief as a lead collaborator once you create a professional brand. It's time to use that brand presence to build the internal network of support that will guide your community into a new culture—a culture of connection. Keep in mind that connection offers benefits and challenges. What are you going to do with both of those facts? How will you convert the benefit you get from establishing trusted connections? How will you convert the benefit you get from your steady development of establishing trusted connections? Don't let challenges thwart your momentum. Turn your attention to your internal school community. It's your place to outreach and teach. Therefore, what's your connecting message? According to Dale McVey, CEO/president of the Ohio School Leadership Academy, and former superintendent of the Hilliard City School District in Ohio, his message is direct and engaging: "Communication is everyone's job in the district. Build it with intention and purpose."

Therefore, if your school district is a place to outreach and teach, model the connecting strategies of networked communication; take Dale's voice to heart. Gather a trusted team of communicative, early amplifiers within your school. You are growing professionally as a lead networker. Don't make that a secret. Be on the lookout for the valuable networks that are blooming in your community in this age of digital and social media and source their support from their own networks. Communication is everyone's job. Network building behavior can go viral in a local way as you lock into this new energy for your community to own. You want the economic theory of "contagion" to work here. Why? It will bring unique energy and momentum. Networking can be satisfying and even fun—it can promote that well-being that is important to any initiative you are engaged in as a school community.

As superintendent, you require internal networks to create the path to change. According to Casciaro, Gino, and Kouchaki (2016),

> Research shows that professional networks lead to more job and business opportunities, broader and deeper knowledge, improved capacity to innovate, faster advancement, and greater status and authority.

Think of a fresh field of new snow and the footprints you are placing on it with this mission to connection. Your footprints make that visible path in the snow and you want to fill that field with more prints. You aren't going it alone! Your stakeholders can follow your steps initially, but you want that field to be full of other paths, their paths that are new and creative to connect those worn from use.

Make this mission joyful for participants, both in the moment of building connections and in the follow-ups that come from sustaining connections. Days, months, years don't matter in making relationships when you have built a strong connection with someone, a connection that binds through the memory you make with them. Our collected internal community has a "neural-biology" wired to keep us connected through emotions. As a leader this is quite a powerful practice to get behind, to be excited about, and to talk up and model. It's a 21st-century active, relational leadership model.

In the past, superintendents have been able to lead in isolation because of a rigid organizational structure that impeded empowerment and shared or distributed leadership. With new tools of digital and social, with the birth of the age of digital information engagement, and with the new awareness of how to manage people in our organizations to get the fullest buy-in and the most shared value, today's superintendents can produce maximum communication impact by modeling networking behavior for those in their community and setting expectations for openness and rewarding stakeholder connectivity.

Superintendents actualize their leadership impact by promoting the value of internal systems full of stories of stakeholder energy. These systems can power collaboration and sustain connected internal school networks. As Seth

Godin says, we live in a connection economy, and your school's internal brand, its personality and its essence, grows through use in exchange with others in the internal organization affirming the connection of the school tribe! Everyone from students to staff, from the third grader to the lunchroom attendant, can feel part of the connected community and can tell the story of the school and its brand every school day. A good feeling in the organization is amplified from being exposed to feelings as people feel safe enough to try to work together without fear, to share with empathy, and to work with authenticity on any task that makes the school a better place to be—a place they want to promote and share.

In any relational school setting, in a hallway conversation, in a department meeting, in a school board session, or during Friday night football, relational power can advance. These human systems sustain networks. The internal systems run on the smallest events linked to stories that keep us in sync when people. Brian Kramer's "human-to-human" networking strategy focuses on what is common to the community. This recognition helps advance relationship building into a priority position in the school organization.

A powerful spark to a successful internal organization is the leader's ability to model collaboration in the community. A more efficient, more communicative internal team results from engaging with the leader's model of continuous collective learning. The impact of this practice touches all stakeholder groups. With a solidly built brand, a leader can inspire a team. There are supportive frameworks to help create growth. Many superintendents have found value in Steven Covey's "Leader in Me" model that recognizes the leadership value in every member of the school community.

Since communication skills are part of leadership, a theme connects internal groups around leadership and communication. The more connected the organization is by its common identified themes, by a brand, or by similar positioning, the more students are likely to have a feeling of belonging to the internal organization and feel more engaged in the learning process. A connected school district has a laser focus on doing whatever it takes to improve student outcomes.

Stakeholders in schools today are likely to welcome a leader's network building plan when this networking behavior is tangible and rewarded. Be present at any moment for celebrating connectivity in the channels you use. Consider your internal communication options: written newsletters, e-mails, Facebook postings, Instagram photos, and old school public relations all show the superintendent's support of a collaborative community and deepen the feeling of connection it brings.

When individuals, partnerships, teams, and departments observe the practice of sharing and are encouraged to give and receive, the dialogue in networks grows. Superintendents learn as business leaders have found in their own internal organizations that it is worth their time to model and design networking systems that bring communities together in multiple ways, online and offline.

If you want your communities to know the value of networking, start strategically to inform them and build awareness. It's the first step in any marketing campaign. First, tell your own networking narrative at every turn to every team you see in-house. Explain how this value has helped in your own growth mind-set, offer real examples in online or real-time conversations of the people you have connected to, who are now members of your valued network, and explain why they are helpful to the school.

Leaders can classify the type of school support these new networking connections bring. In the book *BrandED* the authors encourage you to look at your network and ask yourself about your connections: are they *emotional partners*, simply those contacts who like what you do and who cheer on the community? Are they *service partner*s who will step up and provide value with a servant leadership focus for your school? Are they *product partners* who have the ability to produce resourcing value to the school for needs that help students?

These types of partnerships exist in the internal organization. Thanks to the way the supercharged freelance "gig" economy works, it seems everyone—from a kid in a classroom to a teacher, staff member, or parent—can collaborate and connect in one or more of these supportive ways.

We would also encourage you to read the article "Thriving in the Gig Economy" by Petriglieri, Ashford, and Wrzesniewski. You can access the article by visiting the QR Code below. School superintendents need to recognize that as the economy changes, so will the education sector, which only validates the need for professional leadership networks.

Also, back in Chapter 3, Jeff Allen, a gig Economy Specialist introduced us to Uncle Richard. He is well connected and has a background in education. We encourage superintendents to reach out to him on Twitter (@bjaj1), and LinkedIn (Jeff Allen) to discuss how to transform your school district to align with the new economy.

Many stakeholders have a passionate hustle around their gigs" or side projects that are powerfully impactful and influential. Take advantage of this trend to resource your school. Teach your community to identify connectors among them in the community. Then think about casting that net outward to the external world to find those who fit in one of your three partnership themes. Explain to your community how you are working on new ways to share information in real time and online with partners who can volunteer and offer service or products.

Look for ways to give feedback quickly in engagements with connective partners in texts, in e-mails, or even on social platforms where you can ask questions of the community. Each channel you use in "social media atmosphere" has its own way for you to attract engagement. Don't forget to create a culture of safety and trust in your engagements as you exchange with others in a dedicated effort to network.

OPERATIONAL ALIGNMENT: CALIBRATING THE EXPERIENCE

Internal Networks for Community Growth

A strong leadership brand, discussed in chapter 5, is important to building internal school systems and new dynamic, forward-thinking networks. Without a leader owning his or her own unique leadership brand, and without the clear communication of brand importance to internal teams of teachers, staff, and students, the understanding of the school brand can't be advanced. Internal brand influences the success of building external networks.

Network building is a distributed organizational practice launched by the modeling of a "network-aware" leader whose stated goal is collective and connective communication. Managing administratively modeled peer-to-peer and peer-to-supervisor communication that is clear and respectful can build organization and confidence. With enough modeling, input, and time to practice communication systems, networks can form in-house, reflecting the leadership effort a superintendent models as he or she networks in a way that inspires every member of the school community.

With a connecting message, organizational goals can be met collaboratively, and existing networks can be charged to adopt new ways to communicate and care. People begin to trust and become more open and collaborative if a safe internal environment of connection is modeled by the leader in place. The internal community sees itself as united. Collaborative leadership opportunities can be enjoyed by building internal networks within the school district to advance the overarching school brand, one that will be ready to engage with the new, powerful external networks.

In order to become a networked community, students, teachers, principals, and staff members learn to resource each other, sharing the feeling that they are a valued part of the system. Connective internal communities do the work of developing and communicating the district's core value from their unique perception.

When a system creates brand value together, networks grow organically, and a school organizational trust and belonging results. People who experience a positive collaborative professional networking through brand building go on to build new network connections. Networking is fun, as stated earlier, so take away the feeling of failing that people may place of being a relational stakeholder.

Tell them to simply try connection, no matter if they are introverted or extroverted personalities. As a leader, take the fear of failure away. No one is "bean counting" the number of contacts that are made. Advance your network using a quality-over-quantity lens of relationships. A quick, authentic way to assess if the quality is there happens when people tell you not only what they would miss about you if you were gone but also what they would continue to do in your absence to continue your collaborative legacy.

These new mind-sets for valuing collaborative systems can spark your organization's change to openness. Start calibrating through consistent recognition of the shared values in the internal and external environments. Lose the *internal* US versus *external* THEM attitude; keep welcoming the attitude of a porous networking ecosystem. Give praise and validation to those teachers, staff members, and students who show the interrelatedness of a school community and its culture to the greater, outside world.

There's an energy of "possibility" that networks bring to a school's future. Promoting an open and transparent view of the position that the school holds in its growth as a collaborative community is a foundation for getting people excited and attentive to growing connections. Every day schools can advance internal connectivity through the traditions and routines that are already established.

Through the visual messaging of the school's narrative in hallways, offices, and classrooms, messages about the power of connection and demonstrations of what it looks like become tangible signals: the culture of committing to networking grows in-house. In some schools, this is adopted with vigor in the words of the students displayed on the walls, in the halls, and in offices and common areas.

Student thinking: questions and opinions are displayed and updated regularly. There is nothing more important and more positive to growing an internal network than a leader who models the path by raising his or her voice and shows the way in visibly collaborating, networking, and working in teams to create the sharing of ideas—a focus on "the writing on the wall" with the internal community displaying its personality and brand essence in words, pictures, and videos that get people's attention.

Don't forget to support your teams in the internal system by helping them tell their stories to the community through "content curation." In content curation you behave like an art collector who curates art, but you select and showcase content, stories, and information and then selectively share them across your network online and in real time. Show people the value of this tool, and find those who may already be doing this in their own way in personal networks outside of school.

Understanding internal dynamics is critical to effective leadership, as well as, growing others. We would encourage you to read Glen Llopis' article, "Leadership is About Enabling the Full Potential of Others." Llopis encourages leaders to fully understand their organization and people. Empowering people to grow, to connect (network) with solid mentors who can help grow their abilities as leaders and self-awareness. Read Llopis' full article in *Forbes* magazine by scanning the following QR Code.

When you ask teams to seek out stories that are aligned with their purposes and show them the value online of sharing other reputable pieces of content from other schools or from businesses or from any number of lifestyle sites, you give permission to share and connect. Consultant to higher education, Bart Caylor, publishes regularly about the value of using this strategy, and it is adaptable to our K-12 leadership mission. Original content and curated content keep your brand alive and connected.

Leaders must reflect on a genuine shared story, a narrative that needs to be in place for networking that feeds the culture of collaboration. Take opportunities to listen in your community for the narrative that answers these questions. What is our purpose? Who are we? What is our why? Why do we care? Celebrate the answers to these questions when you see, hear, or feel evidence of this culture on any channel from a tweet to a Facebook post to a newsletter or blog notation—or even a face-to-face handshake of thanks.

When internal school systems promote stakeholder understanding of the school's narrative, the culture and school brand can travel beyond the walls of the school. The community is showing a deeper school brand value—not simply its school spirit. As part of operational expectations, stakeholders can get excited about sharing, and leaders can offer systems that develop new communication skills that break away from insular, ivory tower thinking.

Under the lead of a superintendent who provides the safety to grow professionally using collaborative networks, a feeling of belonging results, and the need to tell the story of the school grows among stakeholders. If they see something positive, they will want to say something! High-performing, collaborative organizations, such as Google and Uber, or any start-up, venture organizations expect collaboration as a means to ignite creativity and innovation—critical components to sustainability. Both creativity and innovation are desperately needed in school districts across the nation today, and networking can help launch a new era of shared creativity in public schools.

Networking mind-sets lead to opportunities that grow a culture of learning within the school district. This change improves the professional practice of teachers. The feeling of security in the belonging that collaboration brings teachers is transferred to students. Both teachers and kids can recognize the value connecting the internal world of teaching and learning with the outside macroenvironment.

The excitement accessing partners outside of the school walls grows among stakeholders who know who they are, who want to share their culture in visual and text engagements, who promote their school stories, and who raise the possibility of finding others who match their culture in near places—the small business in the community—and in far-flung places beyond the school zip code.

Superintendents engaged in professional leadership networks can't help but mentor others into following their lead and develop communication skills that improve overall organizational performance. Today a superintendent who isn't thinking of networking is missing out on opportunities for the future, which will impact student preparation and position the school as a place that is not just keeping pace but setting the trend for the next generation workforce.

We know that most of our students will need to be continual learners after they pick up their diplomas. They will experience constant retraining in jobs almost as soon as they get them because of the pace of change and innovation. The students we have today must be able to pivot through collaboration and team behaviors. We need to give them that soft skill as much as the hard skill tools needed within a discipline.

Internal networks of dedicated storytellers allow school districts to improve efficiency and effectiveness as a living, breathing learning organization. For the district to meet rapid changes and more accountability long term, internal networks of brand-aware participants gain insights and acquire skills that will help the school to succeed. Strategic organizations are led by leaders who are characterized as being lifelong learners who respect a culture of collaborative sharing.

PAUSING FOR TECHNOLOGY: PRACTICAL ADVICE

Tech Strategies for Your Internal Network

Once the community of internal stakeholders—teachers, staff, parents, and students—feel safe in being more open and see the advantage of cultivating their own internal networks in their day-to-day hours in school and outside of school, a superintendent can continually learn as well as lead amply by watching the community connect. Democratization occurs! People who were resistant see the benefit of a shared culture that is always becoming a balance of digital and real-time connection.

It's true that with technology, there is a fear, a disruption, and a loss of productivity as the culture of being open and networked is launched. People need time to grow. Have safety nets of professional development (PD) available for training in digital channels across the internal community. Help people connect at their own level and pace; change can occur without a threat, but keep your eye on the rollout.

These expectations to be transparent may be part of evaluation tools and need to be valued through your leadership. If using a tool like the Danielson model, for example, professional development (PD) is measured through the new professional learning of staff. The building and collaboration through networking can be measured by the adoption and use of new tech tools. Networking for professional growth requires an internal organization culture that encourages collaboration and continuous improvement, and values feedback.

Keep in mind that the segmentation of your ranks from baby boomers to Gen X and millennials sets up the need for opportunities for pairing digital native employees to "mentor up" with their older colleagues in the networks they touch together. Not just formal training but the casual connectivity of setting up networking buddies and partnerships will develop organically for professional learning and networking growth.

Offering value to those who want to step up as lead networkers to promote connectivity is key. How can you celebrate the efforts of your lead networkers? Professional credit? Stipends? Grant access? Resources for their teaching? You are building a future for school connection and an always forward feeling of change. As school superintendent you have an opportunity to create internal change.

When it comes to internal networking, as superintendent, how can you create change? You can follow these four strategies that have resulted in positive changes in school districts. As superintendent, *never work alone*. If the goal is to get others to leave their cubicles, offices, or classrooms, then superintendents must also model this expectation. Venture out of your office, create collaborative spaces in the district office, and work there daily. Invite others to join you at the table to work. These moments of collaboration and teamwork will pay huge dividends down the road.

Create internal professional learning opportunities. Most school districts send staff outside to external professional development (professional development outside of the school district); however, promising and probably better professional learning exist within the district. Think about the possibilities that exists with internal professional learning opportunities. These ongoing activities enable staff to work together, to grow together, and to form internal networks around a common purpose—organizational and professional growth.

Encourage staff members, who are not typically seen as leaders, to lead projects. Superintendents, assistant superintendents, directors, and coordinators are all considered leaders, but what about the specialists and assistants who are often overlooked as leaders? Just think about how empowering it would be for an administrative assistant in the district office to take on the role of the projector leader? This is an excellent networking opportunity to create a sense of internal cohesion. Empowering those who are not typically leaders to be leaders would almost certainly require people to work together so that budgets could be accessed, topical expertise could be garnered, and required sign-offs could occur. Furthermore, teamwork and networking would have to occur as a means to "gel" the work and make sure that the project goes forward.

Learn how to be a connector of dots! Superintendents have a daunting task, especially when it comes to creating an organization that is high performing. Superintendents need to be seen throughout the district as leaders who are willing to work with anyone and at anytime. As the superintendent works with a variety of individuals in the district, connections are made and internal networks form. Working with a variety of people on any given day helps the superintendents become familiar with each person's skills, talents, and expertise, as well as goals and aspirations. Throughout these important points of connections, the superintendent can help others to grow professionally, which, in turn, strengthens the organization's capacity to grow and sustain a vibrant community.

Be the first to recognize others. Praising the work of others, especially during times of success, goes a long way for the superintendent in building a winning and collaborative culture. The ultimate goal of the superintendent is creating internal network unity. A brand foundation of knowing core value results when everyone is working together toward the same goal of creating the best organization for students. When success is reached as a team, everyone should take credit for any level of success. Create a collaborative culture, and those tendencies of "I" will quickly fade to "we" as the team is more important than the individual. Individuals can and should be recognized for their involvement, but the work as a team is really what is being recognized for success.

Internal networks of dedicated storytellers are supported through the many new digital and social platforms that are emerging to help teachers who also feel the aforementioned isolation that superintendents feel. New platforms responding to the research of teacher isolation allow school districts to improve efficiency and effectiveness as a living, breathing, learning organization. The many educator professional learning networks on Twitter have connected thousands of educators around the world.

Entrepreneur Chris Russell, a former Teach for America teacher, and financial professional Enrique Parada, cofounder of Teach for America, are leveraging their Columbia University degrees in a new tech platform called Project 77 that is designed to support the traditional internal system of PD with this best resource model as possible—teachers resourcing each other online! In their program they address teacher isolation and propose digital collaboration and networked community.

Russell and Parada believe the isolation issue in teaching is a vestige of an old attitude of teacher as the sole practitioner responsible for the function of his or her individual classroom. This is seen in the orientation of a teacher's day where 5 percent of his or her time on average is dedicated toward teamwork. Closed classroom doors and lack of collaboration have led to adverse outcomes for both teachers and students.

For a district to meet rapid changes and more accountability long term, internal networks of brand-aware participants gain insights and acquire skills that will help the school to succeed. Strategic organizations are led by leaders who are characterized as being lifelong learners who respect a culture of organizational learning. If a superintendent steps up to the place as a lead networker, the same forecast can be true!

Networking mind-sets lead to opportunities to grow a culture of learning within the school district. Associate Superintendent Valerie Truesdale of the Charlotte Mecklenburg School District in North Carolina identifies learning at the core of this networking effort that is powered by a unique idea of personal growth mind-set for your internal core, "Out of the box thinking, sends the message that all children can grow, all adult learners can grow—a growth mindset must permeate all we do."

This focus on networking builds resources that improve professional practice as teachers. Getting a feeling of security in the belonging that collaboration brings teachers and students recognizes the value connecting the internal world of teaching and learning with the outside macroenvironment. Meshing outside opportunities of collaboration with internal networks adds connective teaching and learning muscle. Superintendents who engage in professional leadership networks can't help but mentor others into following their lead and develop communication skills that can be used to improve overall organizational performance. Today, a superintendent who doesn't understand the value of messaging to new partners is missing the essential part of being a leader today, communication in a local and even global way.

SETTING A PACE: LEADING AS SUPERINTENDENT

Convene. Narrate. Amplify

As complexities mount and schools face an ever-changing student population, superintendents must look for "frictionless" ways to get people "unstuck" and open to engaging in diverse networks that will help them grow their individual mission. Knowing your audience, those who make up the internal landscape of the school community, is key for setting a comfortable pace in developing a networking persona that can meet the unique communication values in the variety of networks in schools populated by diverse cultures.

In leadership we will face challenges as we become transparent and advance a connected agenda. The process of networking contains simplicity and complexity. Celebrate both. In the words of Alan Kay, one of the most prominent computer scientists who pioneered personal computing, "Simple things should be simple. Complex things should be possible." (Merchant, 2017) Pace your networking leadership to possibility. Your pace within your internal system is one of awareness and attraction. Find your early internal networking ambassadors who can aid you in the simplicity of starting. Make networking a team approach, where superintendents and others engage together to build the school narratives and amplify the tangible impact that good networking practices have brought to the community. Then, in collaboration with other peer leaders, districts, and teams, make a shared commitment across your network to cocreate together. Look for chances to promote. Stretch yourself to share brand stories in meetings, events, and casual connections in real time—beyond the usual forum of school sporting events.

Bring people together in a pace that encourages; build everyone's organizational capacity. Enlist all types of people and cultures to make connections as the iconic phrase "all boats rise." Rise together as collaborators. In pacing your in-house efforts, create a culture of learning about many subjects and topics, professional, recreational, and educational, so that unique forms of collaboration can emerge and new ties spark among the most unlikely to be connected. Top companies and organizations have leaders who are continuously looking for opportunities to grow, through internal collaborations around themes and topics outside the daily world of work.

In a fast-paced world, leaders of many of today's top companies use engagement in networks as opportunities to grow professionally internally so that they may form strategic alliances with other leaders that will lead to positive outcomes for their organization.

Leading a small or large company or organization is a difficult job and often very lonely, so pace yourself to find connectivity that will power your efforts and make you a stronger model of relational leadership. Business leaders often use networks as a means to prevent burnout and reduce the loneliness of being at the top. Avoiding burnout is essential to a leader's professional learning plan.

Often, when leaders are exhausted, the last thing that is on their mind is professional growth. They only need relief from the burdens and pressure of the job. Professional networks offer that relief for leaders, and many leaders indicate that preventing burnout is a critical component of having an effective professional learning plan. Many superintendents who do not stay in the profession indicate burnout as one of the top three reasons they leave the profession. Being relational and having a network combats isolation.

Networking power adds welcome relief for superintendents who need to escape the job and focus on their growth as a leader. Superintendents can utilize networks to grow through interactions with others and, more importantly safely learn from others, preventing burnout from occurring. The superintendency is complex and only increasing in complexities as schools are changing daily as a result of an ever-changing world.

Once committed you can continually feed your organization with new networkers as you learn to be comfortable in connecting. Quicken the resourcing by finding natural networkers. Interview them purposefully. Find what makes them remarkable. Hire them in every part of your internal organization. Business leaders recognize that relational talent is key to long-term organizational success. Business leaders are always on the lookout to grow, recruit, and retain top talent as competition is fierce. They create internal networks that will help develop talent that is aligned with not only the business goals and needs but also the employee's needs and long-term goals.

Business leaders use networking as a means to create a culture of learning as a strategic process. The best company leaders encourage collaborative learning through networks as a way to build comradery within the organization and to grow others aligned with long-term strategic goals. Learning throughout the district is often disconnected, with each school leader, teacher, and staff member doing his or her own thing. Through creating internal networks, comradery and collaborative systems form, which can best be described as an internal network. Superintendents can utilize these collaborative systems within the district to provide the best support to take risks, leave their own comfort zones, and begin to collaborate both internally and externally with contacts, colleagues, and partners.

SPOTLIGHTING BUSINESS ACUMEN: PRIVATE SECTOR APPLICATION

Set a goal & be authentic.

—Sabrina Kizzie, MPA, Marketing Consultant
Social Media Adjunct Instructor, Baruch College

I discovered networking has power when I completed graduate school. I was in graduate school doing an internship at a major hospital. My plan was to become an administrator. I was working in a prestigious hospital and was trying to think about how to make my skill set stand out. I met a woman who was a high-level executive, and I asked her to be my mentor. Originally, she said she didn't have time to work with me but was honored to be asked. I didn't give up and kept showing her why it would be beneficial to be my mentor, and eventually she agreed.

The executive began inviting me to networking events with her. We did a buddy system for networking events she invited me to. We would both meet three people and then introduce my three people to her three people. It made the process less daunting and quickly I saw my network grow. She connected me to people within our organization as well as outside of the organization.

Years later, I was up for a job, and I found out that the prospective employer had reached out to a personal contact of her own (not listed on my references) to see if she knew about me. I was surprised to find out her contact was my mentor! Networking has incredible power—both short term and long term.

Today my best strategy is to really truly listen to a new contact when you meet them. What are their interests? What are they looking to accomplish? How can I help them in some way? Listening is a lost art, and the power of being an attentive listener is significant. Before I ask anything of others, I ask, "how can I be a resource to you?" My intent is not to get things from people but be mutually beneficial for both of us.

Meeting people at events and connecting with them directly after by e-mail or on LinkedIn, I am able to follow up with relevant information pertaining to the discussion we had. I will send an article that might be helpful to something we talked about. Set a goal—try to meet with someone once a week. Meet them but don't lose touch. Sometimes we connect on social media platforms and then it remains digital. The best strategy is to maintain that personal connection with follow-up after the initial interaction. We are all busy. The power of that personal connection will yield great fruit and is always worthwhile if you are flexible and committed to make the visit happen.

Building relationships on social media can take some time, but my best advice is to be authentic. For me, I'm a big fan of Twitter. It's helped me connect with a diverse group of people in a quick snapshot. For example, I am able to follow higher education influencers and larger market segment companies that put out great information about higher education. When I like what they are saying, I share their material and read their content, but then I will try to connect with them on LinkedIn and begin to establish a personal connection with that influencer.

Taking the time to develop these connections really sets you up well for the future. I can say from my experience that building relationships on social media has opened up doors for me for speaking engagements and other opportunities. So many people think that a digital connection is just that—connecting online. It's bigger than that. Trish Rubin, in my opinion, is the master of networking. She is the person I turn to for networking advice. Her tagline "All roads lead to Trish" couldn't be truer. She is a force in the networking realm. By the time we finish dinner when we meet, she has already provided multiple e-introductions and has been wonderful about sharing her networking and wisdom with me.

I make it a goal to go to at least one networking event a month. It could be a social media or technology related, but even if it isn't an area of expertise, I will go to meetings of things I'm interested in to create connections. Associations are wonderful because you are able to go as a guest and create contacts across disciplines. Wherever I go, I always make it a point to connect with speakers at events I am attending.

I will try to reach out to them beforehand and then introduce myself at the event. I think it is important for a person to have a platform to connect with people. For me, it's a newsletter. I let them know it's not spamy—it's just a monthly newsletter. I include job postings from my network, places I will be, and so on, and it is a way you can provide "value add" as well as remain connected to your network.

PIVOTING POINTERS FOR CHAPTER 6

- Building networks is not only necessary; it's a career responsibility. Modern-day superintendents understand that collaboration is no longer an option but a critical component of their job in a connected world.
- The good feeling that developed in the internal organization is amplified by visibly modeling a connecting, relational behavior that becomes contagious.
- We live in a connection economy, and your school's internal brand personality, its essence, grows through use in exchange with others in the internal organization who live the brand and affirming the connection of the tribe.
- Today a superintendent who isn't thinking of networking is missing out on opportunities for the future that will impact student preparation and position the school as a place that is not just keeping pace but setting the trend for the next-generation workforce.
- Continually feed your organization with networkers. Quicken the resourcing by finding natural networkers. Hire them in every part of your internal organization. Business leaders recognize that relational talent is key to long-term organizational success.
- Professional networks offer that relief for leaders, and many leaders indicate that preventing burnout is a critical component of having an effective professional learning plan.
- Your pace within your internal system is one of awareness and attraction. Find your early internal networking ambassadors. Make networking a team approach, where superintendents and others engage together to build their narrative and the tangible impact that good networking has brought to the community.
- Bring people together in a pace that encourages sharing to build everyone's organizational capacity; enlist all types of people and cultures to make connections as the iconic phrase "all boats rise."

Intermission: Value-Added *ConnectED Leadership*
Greg Goins

Where do great ideas come from? That's the question that often drove my thinking as I previously served 15 years as a school district superintendent in Illinois. After all, we all want to create innovative, forward-thinking schools that move the needle when it comes to transforming our education systems. But how do we get there? Where do we find those best practices and innovative solutions to create better schools?

My "aha" moment came in 2009 when I started chasing a little blue bird around my computer screen. Once considered an entertainment space to follow celebrities and reality stars, Twitter has now become the epicenter of the education world as school administrators and teachers from around the globe are using specific hashtags to enhance teaching and learning.

As you might expect, this ongoing professional learning has also resulted in some amazing networking opportunities as my own personal journey on Twitter has led me to many of the nation's top school superintendents, principals, teachers, authors, filmmakers, and innovators in education. From those connections, I've discovered many new and innovative ideas that were implemented throughout my school district:

- Joe Sanfelippo (@Joe_Sanfelippo), a superintendent from Fall Creek, Wisconsin, taught me about branding and how to tell your school story with a designated school hashtag.
- Laura Fleming (@LFlemingEDU), a library media specialist, taught me how to turn an old, outdated library space into a thriving makerspace.
- Eric Sheninger (@E_Sheninger) and Tom Murray (@thomascmurray), both innovators in P-12 education, taught me about digital leadership and how to use the Future Ready Schools framework to rethink our school technology plan.
- Kristen Swanson (@kristenswanson), one of the cofounders of the EdCamp movement, introduced me to a better professional development model for my faculty and staff.
- Joe Mazza (@Joe_Mazza), a former principal, taught me the power of Voxer and how to become a "lead learner" in my school district.
- Erin Klein (@KleinErin) and Kayla Delzer (@TopDogTeaching), two outstanding classroom teachers, taught me how to transform our elementary classrooms with flexible seating.

- Jimmy Casas (@casas_jimmy), a former high school principal from Iowa, and best-selling author Jon Gordon (@JonGordon11) taught me the importance of school culture and how to generate more positivity within our schools.
- Ted Dintersmith (@dintersmith), a world leader in education reform, introduced me to his award-winning documentary, "Most Likely to Succeed," and challenged me to think differently about the 21st-century school experience.

As you can see from the aforementioned list, becoming a "connected educator" proved to be a game changer for my school district. It has also allowed me to model digital leadership in ways that I never dreamed possible. From organizing Twitter chats and Voxer groups to hosting my own podcast, the chance to tell great stories and share ideas with a global audience has been one of the highlights of my career as a professional educator.

Today, I'm using those same networking opportunities in my role as full-time professor in educational leadership as I work with current and aspiring school administrators on how to build their very own professional learning network. That's what this chapter is all about—connecting with others and creating better schools for kids.

All you have to do is follow that bird.

ABOUT THE AUTHOR

Dr. Greg Goins serves as director of the Educational Leadership Program at Georgetown College, Kentucky, and spent 15 years as a school district superintendent in Illinois. He is also the host of the popular Reimagine Schools Podcast and is active on Twitter at @DrGregGoins.

Chapter 7

REACHING: Finding Connectivity in Building External Networks

Be genuine. Be remarkable. Be worth connecting with.

—Seth Godin

CONNECTED EDUCATION VIGNETTE: "FIND YOUR CONNECTING FOCUS"

Dr. Richard Thompson, a veteran superintendent of a small school district in the Northeast, has been active in several professional leadership networks during his 15-year career as superintendent. In fact, many superintendents who are close to Dr. Thompson say that he is one of the best "networkers" in the education or at least in their geographic area. Dr. Thompson owns a small business on the side and often attends small business conferences in addition to educational conferences.

Based on Dr. Thompson's resume, experiences, and tenure as a superintendent and small business owner, one would think that he would be engaged in several networks. However, he is active only in two networks that he considers relevant to his career. He is continually being asked by contacts, vendors, other superintendents, and small business owners to be part of various networks; however, he remains committed to the two networks he has been part of for years.

Many superintendents question Dr. Thompson why he would be part of only two professional leadership networks, during a time when collaboration is the catchphrase in education and business. Though many see Dr. Thompson's reluctance to engage in the various networking opportunities as counterproductive, he views his exclusiveness to collaboration as a positive. The networks that he is part of have been in existence for almost as long as

Dr. Thompson has been superintendent. Therefore, the longevity of the network is seen as a plus, considering, like the superintendency, the length of a network is relatively short.

Dr. Thompson strategically participates only in two networks, not because he doesn't think other networks are valuable or worthwhile; he limits his networking as a way to sustain the two networks that he has been part of for so long. He tells other superintendents and business leaders who ask him to join their networks that he wants to focus his abilities on making his two networks sustainable so that future superintendents and small business owners have the opportunity to engage in the positive opportunities of collaboration, collegiality, sharing of ideas, and resources.

Dr. Thompson recognizes his abilities, needs, and priorities, as he limits his networking, as a means to sustain his professional leadership networks that have been so positive in his career and to his district and small business. Dr. Terry often says that overextending oneself, especially during times of collaboration, results in fatigue, effectiveness, and brand damage.

THE NETWORKING PRINCIPLE OF REACHING: PIVOT INTO PRACTICE

Finding Connectivity in Building External Networks

As we head beyond the information age and into a new machine age, the possibility of being released from administrative weight of leading schools through the promise of a combined man and machine workplace environment exists. As we prepare for that time, we can build capacity and acquire skills by actively pursuing broad interests in the microenvironment to create and sustain personal and professional growth. The machines are coming! Actually, they are already here. AI (artificial intelligence) is making organizational tasks easier, so robust networks that give leaders excitement in that feeling of *what's next* in learning can be appreciated.

It is time to pursue new thinking in these kinds of networks that lead a school leader to new strategic partnerships and collaborative opportunities as we move at an amazing pace into the future. Reach is now accelerated. We know that it took the "channel" of the radio to reach an audience of 50 million in 38 years—and it took the channel of Facebook 2 years to hit that same mark of 50 million users. As our networks grow to power our schools, leaders will be agile as the steward of the effort of maintaining networks, internally and externally designed. Sustaining networks is equally as crucial as creating networks. There's a balance, and in many cases, sustaining networks is more critical due to the rate of creation and dissemination of information in this new era.

Vital contacts that are important to the leader's growth and organizational growth and contacts who have become responsible for connecting an educational leader to the wide range of topics that influence a school are valuable and necessary. One objective of developing these varied networks is to showcase school value in new ways to industry and business so that the resourcing of schools by business and agencies who share the same common culture and story can flourish as the example of Dr. Terry shows.

At this point in your growth mind-set, you surely know you need networks, how to create a unique brand value to connect to networks, and how to elevate the urgency to form partnerships internally by your modeling. It's time to strategically tackle that effort of going from local to global, what some networkers call the GLOCAL effort to connect to build your connective culture.

Discipline plays a big part in this as a step in creating connectivity. Finding some initial strategies, both in real time and online, that work for you in local settings of the microenvironment get you started on the journey of building a network of powerful global connectivity for your school. Be encouraged to look across "verticals" of industry for ideas about what is taking place: for example, in finance, Bitcoin; in the automotive industry, self-driving vehicles; in the hospitality industry, robot concierges; in food, insects for lunch.

There is much to educate yourself about and to share as you build your network. Take a page from a successful Madison Avenue advertising agency, sparks & honey, and develop your network as it does with a keen eye toward finding thought leaders across many topics who can open the world to new thinking to their own professional development as well as the development of their schools' connectivity.

The world of thought leaders is a click away on your keyboard. Remember it's a DIY and IKEA effect world; you can form relationships with select thought leaders or simply listen in on their open content and learn from them for free. Start small but keep a routine. Set Google alerts for big ideas and topics in education and beyond. Allow yourself time to simply roam the landscape of the platforms and see which has a fit for your needs, goals, and aspirations.

Make time in your day to read short posts and articles and watch quick videos. On seeing or hearing an interesting voice in any field, add it to your list of possible networking connections. Search through Google and find their preferred channel of communication. Start to follow them and notice their content. Listen and learn! Gradually you can make connections in the channel you are most comfortable in that will lead to professional growth and new and even stronger existing networks. Twitter is a great place to start, and in the appendix you will learn actionable tips on how to get set there, and with other channels from our digital expert and former New York City principal, Judith Wilson.

You also have peers who can validate your content online through sharing, and you will do the same in a reciprocal activity. Go beyond liking and retweeting and make comments to your network partners online. As Dr. Steve Johnson, superintendent of the Lisbon Public Schools District 19, has found,

Both formal and informal networks are necessary to build lasting connection. From formal state organizations to friendly circles of neighboring superintendents, to new connections on social media, leaders can thrive and collaborate. Social media opened up a whole new network for Dr. Johnson as a rural superintendent in North Dakota.

Once you set about the job of showing yourself as an engaged networker in a variety of circles, the greater community can engage with you in support of effort and even help mitigate against risk as you act with increased transparency. A big part of what holds leaders back is the fear of risks that creates open borders that bridge them with external sources of value. Value exists in cross-industry fields of science, business, media, and health.

In the 19th century, there was also fear of innovation during the manufacturing age. A group known as Luddites openly rebelled out of fear to the changes in 19th-century manufacturing technology. Fear comes with disruption and innovation. Move beyond it; lose the Luddite view of tech change in your external network. It isn't a badge of honor in this connected time.

According to Dr. Yee Wan, the Director of Multilingual & Humanities Education Department for the Santa Clara County Office of Education and Past NABE President:

> "As an educational leader, I cherish professional network members as my primary thought partners. Not only do professional networks provide a safe place for me to share ideas and tackle problems, the network members' expertise and feedback prove valuable in helping me reflect on my practices and grow as a leader. Educational leaders will surely benefit from such participation and experiences."

What does a fledgling macroenvironment of connected networks look like? Think about this: a professional leadership network that involves the city mayor, chamber of commerce director, hospital executive, judge, or small business leaders is a place to start. No one knows this better than Dr. Jeffrey Collier, Michigan superintendent of Au Gres School District, who does a regular podcast with his city manager, John Stanley, who is featured as a business voice in our text.

Start at the local level with a path you can easily access face-to-face, and present yourself in your new leadership brand to new contacts in the community. Following that, offer the expansion into online relational behavior by sharing links in e-mails to those in your network or texting a critical new piece of info that they might connect with in their own work. It is a deliberate process and a conscious effort.

The superintendent's capacity to sustain these multifaceted networks requires critical contacts in the network to understand the value they bring to directly impacting the school district. According to Jarillo and Ricart (1987), networks exist through real-life cooperative arrangements. Having a call list, a routine that asks you to access a set number of contacts a day through digital messaging that leads to a face-to-face connection, is part of planning for connection. Particularly in small school districts, superintendents must recognize the value and the importance of sustaining partnerships with key government and community leaders as resources are scarce and shared.

Professional leadership networks need tending. According to Sunseri and Kosteva (1992), most leaders find sustaining a network a time-consuming process that requires a focus on the details. Superintendents must realize that once they become active in networks, data such as phone numbers, e-mail addresses, organizational information, and interests will be important, but as we know, there are many new ways that are embedded into social media like group and list function, relieving a leader of that stress. These rote tasks given to AI over the next years will free leaders to focus on the relational touch that keeps a connection alive.

Using basic tools that are digital aids has helped Neerja Punjabi, principal of the James P. Grieve School, in Caledon, Ontario, to become connected to stakeholders. She seeks new ways to communicate with parents knowing a majority of the parent community are of the millennial generation and have access to smartphones and devices. Because it is critical to build healthy and positive relationships to network with parents and extended community partners, Neerja knew the school reputation and credibility would have to be built on a solid ground. They had to use technology to their advantage and found ways to reach out to the community without using the traditional ways of communication. She chose a new method that was convenient and accessible to reach out to the entire community. A digital tool like SMORE allows her to create instant newsletters that can be shared by sending a link through Synnervoice.

OPERATIONAL ALIGNMENT: CALIBRATING THE EXPERIENCE

Resourcing External Networks

As school districts across the nation face challenge, the rise of innovative competition, stagnant budgets, and an increasing teacher shortage, sustaining professional leadership networks is a part of the long-term strategic focus. From the start, superintendents should think about how they can get across the point that they care. Showing empathy is a powerful part of creating connectivity.

Show that you care about those you build networks with by being generous with your time and content. Show your care about sustaining trust across networks, contacts, and strategic partnerships. Sustaining a network must begin by deciding "why?" Judge which networks to participate in and why they are beneficial for your networking development; then dedicate yourself to the "care and feeding" of the systems.

One such school district that takes this charge seriously is Tennessee's Hamilton County Schools, which, when inspired by a model of business connectivity, learning, and networking, created its own model called Leadership Chattanooga. Its school/community version is an example of disruptive thinking. It's an effort aimed at getting community members involved in the district to increase the effectiveness and boost the number of education advocates, https://tinyurl.com/y7qxx8oz.

As mentioned in previous chapters, the superintendent finds ways to engage in networks that are relevant to his or her needs, goals, strategic interests, or the organization's needs or goals. If the network is not relevant, the chances to sustain a network will be difficult, if not, impossible. The network must have a meaning for the superintendent and the district, and the value and care of that relationship should be obvious. Why engage in a network that will not add value to the leader's brand, performance, or the district's long-term sustainability? Engaging in a network just so that you can say you are part of a network, or without a shared commitment, is not effective.

According to McCarthy (2006), trust is the bedrock not only to an effective network but also to the sustainability of a network. Today, leaders realize that a network is an ever-growing circle of new contacts: friends, partners, colleagues, and like-minded members of the same community or communities at a distance. As the superintendent is typically seen in the community as the chief educator and often sits on several community boards, he or she must be trustworthy. Trust becomes important to leveraging and growing networks outside of the school since new relationships with institutions, new peers, or influential people will take time to grow.

The trust that leaders have built up in the community also adds value to their extended network and, more importantly, the sustainability of the network. A perfect example of this is Alberto Carvahlo, superintendent of Miami-Dade County Public Schools, who has worked tirelessly to build partnerships with local businesses, community organizations, and elected leaders to help Miami-Dade County Public Schools experience a transformation on several levels over his tenure, specifically in student achievement, graduation rates, and college admission.

Superintendent Carvahlo is a person that we encourage you to follow on Twitter using his Twitter handle @miamisupt. Many of his tweets focus on building on the trust he has in the Miami community—his school brand message, "A promise made, a promise kept," reiterates his commitment to the partnerships he has built in the community to move the district forward. He sends the message that trust and partnerships are vision critical to helping the district to continue to work for students!

If no one in the network is seen as trustworthy and no one in the network trusts each other, the level of collaboration, sharing of strategies and resources, and creation of opportunities to speak candidly while seeking advice on how to handle situations will be nonexistent. This makes the life of building the network short. It goes without saying trust, especially in education, among the superintendent, district, and the community is priceless. The level of trust the community (tax payers, business owners, parents, elected officials) has on the school district impacts school funds, student success, and countless other concerns.

Engaged school superintendents actively work to keep their network active and moving forward. Professional leadership networks remain active, relevant, and adaptable to leaders' needs by being open and transparent. Professional leadership networks should not be handled or organized as some secret society. In fact, to sustain professional leadership networks, transparency is vision critical to the growth of the leader, the network, and also the organization that the leaders represent.

A professional leadership network is considered to be engine of strategic marketing. This kind of attitude powers the school beyond the local into the more global possibilities of new networks. As mentioned earlier, school districts are free in today's connected world to market their unique brand. A superintendent today builds a unique personal professional brand characterized by effective leadership, empowerment, vision, and empathy.

A network helps to market the district brand and position the leader positively, and network members take true pride in doing so. According to Farthing (2010), networks need recognition; they need to be celebrated for their work and their focus on an organization and community. If the network is never publicly recognized and simply operates behind a veil, its purpose is not fully understood or appreciated and participation can be threatened.

Sustaining a network is as important as creating a network or becoming part of the network. From time to time, school system leaders will find that some networks are not suited to their or their organization's needs and goals and will have to disengage. However, most professional leadership networks will be beneficial and thus will need to be sustained. Sustaining a professional leadership network is somewhat based on the level of newness leaders can generate from time to time.

Commit to being agile and flexible as you build and connect. Professional leadership networks require a certain level of adaptability so that the network remains relevant. According to Fredricks (2003), for networks to be successful they need true relationships, shared information, and commitment to maintenance. Fredricks claims that for a network to be a professional leadership network, it is not a one-time meeting. The relationship is built to exist over time and to be maintained. He suggests leaders choose networks wisely and be willing to put forth the effort to ensure the sustainability of the network. Keeping it real seems to be a check on expanding networks!

According to Willem and Lucidarme (2014), trust and network flexibility are often found to impede the overall success of the professional leadership network. School superintendents must understand that they must work to ensure that collaboration and network flexibility go hand in hand. Professional leadership networks must adapt to the diverse and changing needs of a continually changing superintendency. The key to both is that the superintendent engage in the development of network processes and also clearly communicate changes as they occur, if any, in regard to goals, needs, supports, and so on.

School superintendents need to practice what is known as "scalable learning" by growing their connected networks through an ongoing continuous acquisition of critical friends, professional relationships, and opportunities to keep them growing and sharing information as their job increases in complexity. Over time, the importance of sustaining these key contacts and opportunities to collaborate will become invaluable to the learning of the superintendent and the school district.

School superintendents are collaborative role models in their districts, so connecting behavior can spread in a balance of face-to-face and digital networking. Be careful though, as the excitement of discovering new social networks can be exhilarating. You will be a wonderful model for "Eyes up. Phones down" behavior if you keep your social media connecting in check on a daily basis, even with phone in hand.

Assure your H2H networking has a strong face-to-face component for your school to benefit. Of course, your networks will be digital and social, but practice "on your feet" management by walking around, modeling interest in balanced connection for your internal community. In this position, leaders increase their chances of networking being valued. The more school superintendents are seen in the district on their feet collaborating with other leaders, teachers, staff members, parents, and community and business leaders, the more others in the macroenvironment will be willing to do the same. Collaboration and networking must be seen in the district as vision critical and working in isolation as a "thing" of the past. Superintendents have little time in today's environment to not work with others.

According to McIntyre (1999), these effective teams of collaboration are characterized by possessing "strategic goals, extensive networks, collaborative relationships, effective information processing, and focused action" (p. 40). Extensive networks, formed both internally and externally, help align the organizational focus and vision going forward, while creating opportunities for empowerment.

Empowerment helps organizations grow, and school districts are no different. School superintendents tending both external and internal networks have an opportunity to help others to step into leadership roles in ways that will power connection of the school community with a wide variety of diverse networking partners. Schools with a clearly defined brand have acquired the essential skills to communicate effectively.

As Ted Fujimoto reminds us in his introduction to this text, the power of the internal brand in a microenvironment, as represented in the brand of the Ritz-Carlton hotel, "ladies and gentlemen serving ladies and gentleman," sets the course for an overall, collaborative brand presentation demonstrated by every member of the organization to customers and stakeholders as they tell their story of service. A school team can do the same in one collaborative protocol using a connecting voice as it presents its brand to the external networks it serves each day.

These networks are empowered to tell their story in traditional and new age ways. Hopkins and Higham (2007) suggests that for an organization to be effective people must collaborate and work well together toward a common goal. Hopkins and Higham (2007) also suggest that effective teams and collaboration lead to leadership opportunities and the empowerment of others. When looking out across potential partners and supporters, A superintendent must trust the work of engaged internal networks that are empowered to expand partnerships and contacts for the school, which ultimately will be transformative for the school district. Empowerment leads to the belief that today's school districts can be in control of their stories and the path to resourcing and support. Instead of being plagued by working in silos, schools celebrate connection.

PAUSING FOR TECHNOLOGY: PRACTICAL ADVICE

Listen—Then Listen Over and Over

Reach out as a leader in this tech-driven work where billions of people are connected on mobile phones through powerful social platforms: two billion alone on Facebook. Throw open the doors to a connected community beyond the school. The world is readying itself for the students in our classrooms as creators and consumers in a new age where we will collaborate with machines as well as people, and our networks will eventually include that learning from the machines which will be part of our networks.

When thinking about what's next, cast a wide net and read into platforms that can offer you these views. One rule of building external networks is to operate out of the belief that there are smart people who understand technology in our school communities, and they may be unlikely experts who can help us to better position our students beyond test scores to life. Thanks to YouTube and Google, people have resourced themselves to levels of tech skill that can be of value to our community.

Find your tech tribe, and appeal to them to offer you support; engage them with your internal networks to go beyond your comfort level to make friends in technology. Start your quest to connect to thought leaders, businesses, and platforms by auditing your community. What skills do they have that they are willing to share with you as a connected leader? As you follow this path, keep your eye out for influencers, people online with strong followings whom you can follow and then connect with to create possible school partnerships. These influencers are in your own internal systems as well as in the external spaces.

"Imagine my surprise," Trish Rubin shares, "when I learned that a young French MBA student in my own Baruch Brand Management class was an impressive millennial fashion influencer with over 100,000 followers online on Instagram—and I was her marketing teacher!" Be humble when it comes to sourcing out help. Many of our students and teachers can "mentor up" and help the more senior members of the school achieve connectivity.

There's never been a better time to bring people into the digital tent, in the words of Superintendent Kristine Gilmore of D.C. Everest School District in Wisconsin; the call to action is simple, "Support the dreams of the student—this is the way to do it." For Trish, the student's "thank-you" was found in the course through understanding how traditional tools can work with new age tools. She supported the dreams of her student in the United States where she wanted to extend her influence. Trish took note of her student's growing presence and learned too!

Gather a collective whose collaborative impact with tech skills can resource your effort. Once you have shared your new brand of collaborative model for networking, you will be able to tell your story and set a learning pace in front of any segment of the community. Keep your pace. It's not the best practice to go from being siloed to superconnected. That's not a real track to building presence. Start with the few select channels that we've described in the chapters and in the appendix and find your digital mentors.

Start small, but start. What will you talk about when you start to broadcast your thinking to the world in order to connect? Take a chance. Even trying out the voice messaging feature on LinkedIn can get you feeling comfortable broadcasting your voice. It gives you a one-minute window to leave a message. Even just a short 30 seconds of saying "hi and hope your day is going well" or commenting on an article or asking for assistance can be done in this personalized way. Head to your LinkedIn message and hold down the microphone button! Look to the common elements that people look for, shared celebrations, check out the Google Days of the Year Calendar. On that alone you could create connections any day of the year to finding people to connect with and things to tweet, post, and photograph.

Aggregators of news are also a great resource. Beyond your Twitter or Facebook feed, look at other worlds, other external communities, and find the quickest way to get information to share or comment on or write about. An example is the newsletter Finimize, which can get leaders up to speed in three-minute daily reads about the world of finance, the news about money, the trends, the discoveries. Want to be informed about block chain? As a school leader you should be. Connecting to a daily read around those topics such as cryptocurrencies can grow you connected brand presence. Check out the Wise Geek or Curiosity platforms, and then post their content to share for comments. Look into the various marketing content platforms or business platforms like *Forbes* and Business Insider; connect to the millennial platforms of Mashable and Bustle. Listen in!

After going out in those curation waters, get your internal team involved and have them find the same resourcing power and connection to the external world by sparking their creativity. Show them you are excited about connections, and you want to know what they are seeing. It's a bit of trend spotting that the aforementioned sparks & honey agency does do well. It looks at trends. The best partners for this are the millennials and Gen Zs in your school, but don't discount retirees or stay-at-home dads or moms who can help the school find the next partner to help them resource through their own.

Keep beating the drum on "listening"—always listening to the beat of content on social media. Keep informed by what you see, and share it with your teams. Ask them what they think of a post; start a conversation. Schools with closed networks can be treasure troves of trends that are impacting schools from the outside. When you are bold enough as a model, launch your own # and create a twitter chat.

As you will see in chapter 9, it's easy to do when you know what the platform is, what it means, and why you should care about it. Even if only a few people show up to talk about the questions you post, you are showing your skill at being a transparent social and digital leadership presence. The saying from *Field of Dreams*, "If you build it they will come," works even with social media. You may start small, but make sure that you have a daily presence on the many social media avenues—before you know it, you will have a following. Scott Levy, CEO and founder of Fuel Online, as well as a best-selling author, provides excellent information about social media content. We have provided his article from *Entrepreneur* magazine; check it out.

Add practice to your tech presence on a select channel with the intention to upgrade your video presence that can be found as authentic and interesting to potential partners for your school. If you are experimenting with Facebook live, start with posting a casual "talking-head" style of video in a selfie moment about a school event and how you are looking forward to attending. Then move over to your Twitter and write a post to the event with a link to the occasion followed with a few school hashtags. Tag in a few peers from your network who are on Twitter, and you will be pivoting to new power as a tech user.

SETTING A PACE: LEADING AS SUPERINTENDENT

See Yourself as a Networking A.C.E.

Start slowly as you approach the world of networking with the external world, and do it well. Have a plan in place that comes from the recognition of who you want to meet, what value you can give, and how you want to engage with them to the benefit of both. Integrate your plan with attention to new contacts in real time by pushing yourself to find new places to meet, to learn, and to socialize that are out of your comfort zone. Once in these places, you can test your personal brand going beyond an elevator speech and giving what business thought leader Simon Sinek refers to as your WHY. Why you do what you do, not simply what you do.

Remind yourself of *quality over quantity*. They are both part of the networking mix as Duckworth told us in chapter 3, but for pacing, the aspect of identifying the quality contact should be at the top of the mind. So many people have paid online to boost their connections to what end? You don't need a wealth of contacts; you need the right contacts. Your internal networks can help you keep that pace and build confidence.

Your internal networks can also work with you to connect with the same networks. What is a peer contact for you could be an aspirational contact for someone on your team. Practice being generous by connecting these contacts to others you know. Connect the dots! When that happens, you are flexing your connector muscle: it means that you will have reached a top behavior in a networked professional community.

By inviting two people to connect, you practice the value of your own brand that is shared in a trusted connection. This practice is a good pace for refreshing yourself. If the current professional leadership networks you have become monotonous, look to collaborate more strategically and regularly in diverse networks, while making new connections that will strengthen your network.

Share that in a big way as a means to be seen as generous; instead of viewing collaboration in professional leadership networks as a necessity, view collaboration with new partners as a strategic process to create new opportunities to grow, learn, and diversify ideas. By making introductions you bring more people to the decision-making table and new ideas in the organization and open the door to new partnerships that can strengthen the district's leadership and organizational effectiveness and lead to more empowerment of others.

Finally, a simple strategy that has worked for Trish Rubin, since 2007, and has been a model for her work as she comfortably works at the intersection between business and educational leadership. This strategy has been written about in both business articles and educational pieces. Use this simple structure. *Ask yourself every day if you are a connectED ACE.* By being a "connectED ACE" every day, you will simply capture the essence of the six chapters of this book. ACE stands for ASSOCIATE, CREATE, and ENGAGE. And all three terms help you to grow purposefully as a networked educator:

ASSOCIATE: The act of associating is a daily exercise in employing the tools; we have both face-to-face and online to share your professional brand with new and known connections. Leaders need practice in associating—flexing the relational muscle. All internal and external stakeholders are on your relational radar every day using any routines, tools, and practices that keep you connected.

CREATE: It is a superintendent's job to be a creator: a creator of interest, a creator of content, a creator of online and real-time activities. Think of yourself with a marketer's view! Experiential marketing is big in our brand world. What experiences can you and your team create that keeps your network looking for you?

ENGAGE: See yourself as the leader of an educational hub that once it has created interest engages through stories, sharing, and bonding. Engage for continuing powerful relationships.

Now every day as you open the door to your office, think: *how will I "ACE" my network today as I associate, create, and engage for my brand and my school's brand?* When you leave that night, close the door and reflect: *how did I crush it today as a connectED ACE?*

This steady attention to being relational will bring reward to you as the lead networker of your community. And if being a connectED ACE appeals to you, and you are a tech-savvy owner of an AI assistant, use your Alexa AI to help you curate information through a daily FLASH BRIEFING that can give you regular daily doses of curated content helping your ACE. Just say to ALEXA, "Give me my Flash Briefing," as you sip your morning coffee, and you will be connected to news and focused content that you select to get you ready to connect with your internal and external networks.

SPOTLIGHTING BUSINESS ACUMEN: PRIVATE SECTOR APPLICATION

> Be purposeful and emotionally intelligent.
>
> —Annalie Killian, Vice President, Strategic Partnerships
> at sparks & honey Agency
> Madison Avenue, NYC

I discovered networks had power at a young age. I started doubling my network at age 12 on completion of primary school in South Africa. I figured if I didn't follow all my primary school mates to the same designated high school, but opted for another, I could immediately double my network of friends! Long before Facebook, when I was in high school, we had things like international pen pals with whom we'd exchange snail mail letters—so starting with that experience at a young age, I had international pen pals. I am still in touch with them!

After completing high school in South Africa, I traveled to Australia as a Rotary Youth Exchange Student and exploded my international network. I also did a lot of volunteering and leading clubs and events at university, which further helped my social networking skill. From that experience, I soon learned the secret for me was "put your hand up to lead." The moment you lead, you rise from the crowd and become visible and memorable.

You can do the same today in a fast-paced digital world. Be purposeful and emotionally intelligent when seeking a digital connection with someone you don't know. When making those first connections on LinkedIn or other platforms, take the time to write a short and relevant note; demonstrate interest in the other's work, and offer how a connection could be mutually symbiotic rather than focusing on your own needs and interests. Pique THEIR interest!

My mum gave me her dog-eared copy of Dale Carnegie's *How to Win Friends and Influence People* when I was in high school. Its tip for remembering people's names once introduced is solid gold! I also gained a great deal of benefit from studying various personality profiling systems like Myers Briggs, Enneagram, and DISC as well as Professor B. J. Fogg's Persuasion Model.

Today I actively pursue broad interests—culturally, I attend all sorts of events and the theater and read broadly way beyond the disciplines that I studied formally. This makes it easy to start conversations with just about anyone I come across. And I always talk to new people when I travel or attend events. Airports and planes are fabulous places for serendipitous connections. Also, I say "yes"—a lot!

PIVOTING POINTERS FOR CHAPTER 7

- Engaging in networks is critical for veteran and aspiring leaders.
- Networks help to improve the overall organizational performance—as leaders connect with other leaders and their effectiveness improves.
- When embraced and utilized effectively, networks help to focus the organization on its mission, vision, and long-term strategic goals.
- Networks help to expand and sustain the pool of transformative leaders.
- Diversity in connections only leads to a stronger and more sustainable network.
- Maintaining networks is critical for new and aspiring leaders (Gabriel and Farmer, 2009).
- Tapping into the diverse experience of leaders helps maintain networks (Dulworth, 2008).
- Listen on social media, and find your topics that can lead to new connections.
- Build a file of thought leaders to aspire to connect with, and show your connection to them through appreciating their content.
- Use the ACE strategy to simply develop your daily networking muscle. Learn to ASSOCIATE, CREATE, and ENGAGE each day to grow your efforts; then model and teach this behavior to your team.

Chapter 8

BELONGING: Supporting Systems and Frameworks That Sustain a Networking Strategy

Belonging has always been a fundamental driver of humankind.
—Brian Chesky

CONNECTED EDUCATION VIGNETTE: NETWORKS LEAD TO BELONGING

Networks Lead to Belonging

Mr. Roger Dunham, a new superintendent of a large city school, was once chief executive officer of a large educational technology company before becoming superintendent. Mr. Dunham joins a growing number of his peers who are becoming superintendents after leading private sector companies or serving as officers in the military. Mr. Dunham, unlike many of his colleagues, brings a unique experience and views into the chief executive officer position of a school district.

Taking over the position of superintendent of schools, he worked quickly to create a sense of belonging among all stakeholders in the district. Mr. Dunham saw himself as an outsider who lacked educational understanding but understood organizational theory. Instead of focusing on what he didn't know, he focused on creating an organization that valued employing other viewpoints, primarily through internal and external networks.

Mr. Dunham wanted everyone to feel as if they were part of the decision-making process. In his former role as a vice president of strategy for a local pharmaceutical manufacturer, he worked with staff within his department to build partnerships with other departments, local pharmacists, and physicians and regularly helped group listening sessions with patients. At the time, many viewed Mr. Dunham's focus on interactions with internal and external stakeholders as time consuming; as sales and customer satisfaction began to increase, others became convinced of Mr. Dunham's logic.

The goal was not only to increase sales but also to make sure that everyone from his team to the local pharmacist and ultimately the consumer felt as if they were part of the company and decision-making process. They were, in other words, vested in the success of the company. Mr. Dunham wanted to do the same thing with the local school district, as he was vested in their success. Two of his children attended one of the district's elementary schools, and another attended one of the middle schools. He wanted the district to succeed so that his children would have the best learning opportunities.

Mr. Dunham fully understood, better than most, that stakeholders, everyone from the custodians to bus drivers to the local business owner and ultimately the student belonged to something; they would work to make the district better. Since there were no structures in place to encourage networks, Mr. Dunham was determined to get structures in place so that everyone had a voice at the district level.

Mr. Dunham's commitment to networking resulted in one of the most successful local networks of stakeholders that met regularly and helped create a long-term strategic plan based on student voice, business partnerships, and internal collaborative constructs. Not only did student achievement increase, but stakeholder perception of the district also became more favorable, and the networks expanded to other sectors of the community and helped increase diversity in the decision-making process in the district.

THE NETWORKING PRINCIPLE OF BELONGING: PIVOT INTO PRACTICE

Supporting Systems and Frameworks That Sustain Networks

Empowerment always leads to empowerment, one of the few times that the "trickle-down" theory works. As superintendents empower others to be leaders, empowerment extends all the way down to students. Empowerment does lead to the expansion of empowerment and in some cases the inspiration to do something great—which is the hope of all educators when it comes to the empowerment of students.

Today's school superintendents are dealing with a variety of issues that superintendents 5–10 years ago would not fathom but are now called on today to address. As mentioned previously, to tackle the complex issues in today's schools, school superintendents must look to create an organization with collaborative leadership constructs that foster shared decision-making.

Professional leadership networks help to empower not only the superintendent but others in their roles, no matter the position. Empowerment leads to a more collaborative culture. According to Spreitzer (2017), collaboration leads to individual empowerment, and networks are vital to creating an organization that is empowering. The modern-day school district, as an organization, needs more collaboration and empowerment, not less.

We have talked about the fact that after decades of isolation the days of school superintendents, directors, and coordinators working solo in their offices and cubicles in isolation are over. The complexities that school districts face today are getting to the heart of leading; changing leadership from within is key. Communicative empowerment has a lot to do with the new collaborative style of superintendents and the school districts.

In today's districts success is found by moving from operating in silos to operating through collaborative leadership structures. Carson, Tesluk, and Marrone (2017) found that the internal culture of an organization led to the emergence of a shared purpose and external coaching were significant predictors of performance.

Superintendents who engage in networking behavior bring heightened alertness to the organizational performance and model how to bring others into leadership roles. Network connectivity builds capacity in superintendents. By engaging with the practice of fellow superintendents who have successfully empowered others and restructured an organization by using networks, they feel more comfortable and inspired to do the same in their school districts.

Keller and Dansereau (1995) argue that the leader sets the tone for the organization. Keller and Dansereau cite that many school districts rise and fall based on the style, performance, and vision of the superintendent—all the more reason to connect. The superintendent is the gatekeeper to empowerment and creation of a culture of collaboration in the organization. Empowerment is more than just a process; it's a mentality and an essential component found in a superintendent's leadership style and organization.

Through participating in internal networks grown in the district, superintendents can gain a better understanding of employees' roles, job functions, needs, goals, and aspirations. Knowing this and being actionable to provide support strengthen the zone of empowerment within the school district. Many superintendents utilize zones of empowerment as a strategic process to empower others based on organizational needs and professional needs.

The result of a superintendent's collaboration with other superintendents in professional leadership networks is essential. Through connectivity, superintendents grow the ability to acquire the skills and strategies needed to empower others to be strategic leaders in the school district. Imitation is a high form of praise, and much can be learned from peers, which leads to action. Sharing of information is a critical component in both collaboration and empowerment, as knowledge is power.

Empowerment continues to be emphasized in literature but is noticeably absent in network discussions for superintendents. However, the need for superintendents to recognize the need for empowerment and have a full understanding of the many facets of empowerment in school districts grows in importance. School districts must transform, from rigid organizations with strict and hierarchical leadership structures to more flexible organizations with collaborative leadership structures.

According to McIntyre (1999), effective teams are characterized by "strategic goals, extensive networks, collaborative relationships, effective information processing, and focused action" (p. 40). Extensive networks, both internally and externally, help align the organizational focus and vision going forward, while creating opportunities for empowerment. Empowerment, in fact, helps the organization to grow, and school districts are no different.

As we have shown, school superintendents use both external and internal networks to help others to step into leadership roles and acquire the essential skills to lead effectively. At the end of the day, however, networks encourage collaboration, which leads to empowerment. According to Hopkins (2003), for a network to be effective, people must collaborate and work well together. Hopkins et. al (2008) further adds that effective teams and networks lead to leadership opportunities and the empowerment of others.

As superintendents engage in networks, they are empowered. Empowerment leads to a connective belonging—a belief that today's school districts must be collaborative instead of being plagued by isolation. Those school district leaders who miss this message will find it challenging to be empowered or empowering others in their roles.

ORGANIZATIONAL ALIGNMENT: CALIBRATE THE EXPERIENCE

Supporting Collaboration

Collaboration in organizations is one of the most important strategies for long-term success. Household company names such as Apple, Google, Ford, General Electric, and Facebook possess a culture of belonging, which fuels collaboration. Bringing people together and then creating a culture of collaboration is vision critical to an organization and more importantly to the overall effectiveness of organizational leaders.

According to Rahman, Endut, Faisol, and Paydar (2014), collaboration encourages the following in organizations: (1) creativity, (2) cooperation among team members with diverse backgrounds, (3) sharing of information, (4) quality of the product being developed, and (5) overall service quality. Finally, collaboration leads to improvements in the communication between team members and the organization. According to Muijs, West, and Ainscow (2010), networking and collaboration have become an important focus in education.

Due to the complexities that educators face, collaboration and networking often face barriers. There are many constructs that superintendents will have to address as they look to begin the journey to networking, with the hope of a culture of collaboration. Some of the constructs are time, schedules, costs, understanding, and willingness of school superintendents and system leaders to value the concept.

In chapter 5 we argued that external professional leadership networks provide superintendents, district leaders, and other members of the school district an opportunity to establish critical partnerships with the community and business organizations. Transformative superintendents recognize and model that belief that innovative collaboration helps organizations to build stronger relationships with the communities they serve.

Evidence of the value of innovative collaboration removes the constructs that often prevent internal and external stakeholders from partnering and collaborating with district leaders. In marketing terms, get activated! Activations in marketing are the planned visible evidence that something special is happening that is building communities. Ever been to a festival? A street fair? Ever enter a contest online? These are marketing opportunities known as activations that create interest and result. Ever been to a school football game? A play? A science fair? See the connection. Empower your community through existing channels that you treat as connecting brand and networking opportunities.

As students' needs change, societal expectations change, so must school districts. According to Martins and Terblanche (2003), creativity and innovation are critical to the existence of an organization moving forward. We would add that collaboration with the greater school community is vision critical to the district as an organization. Without partnerships with internal and external players, school leaders are destined to fail as silos impede growth, outreach opportunities, and empowerment.

Within school districts, collaboration and strategic networks with businesses, organizations, and governments are critical to the long-term success of the school district. Professional leadership networks can be the conduit that forms these important opportunities for collaboration and joint success that can lead to greater success for the district and the community. According to Díaz-Gibson, Civís-Zaragoza, and Guàrdia-Olmos (2014) collaboration through networks assists school districts in addressing a broad range of social issues.

In today's school districts, there must be a set of shared goals, based on a unifying vision for the district and student success. These strategic plans are perfect for adding collaboration and networking goals. Too often, district leaders, school leaders, teachers, staff members, parents, and the community are all working hard to help students but many times in silos. According to Moolenaar, Sleegers, and Daly (2012), there must be a collective efficacy within the district, based on mutual goals. Ultimately, collaboration leads to shared leadership within the district, where all stakeholders are empowered to be leaders. Professional leadership networks, both internal and external, can be the creative conduits to helping form a shared purpose throughout the district.

Develop a culture of collaboration and not just a list of talking points. School superintendents have a responsibility, especially in today's culture of high-stakes testing, stagnant budgets, and increasing teacher turnover, to find the stabilizing factor—connection can be that factor. Successful superintendents regularly take the lead and engage in open collaboration with other superintendents, principals, teachers, parents, and community members.

This collaboration is achieved through strategic, concise, and relevant networking with the aim of growing the district and improving the organization's performance and ability to meet the diverse needs, goals, and aspirations of students. A strategic approach to collaboration and sustainable networks does not occur through sporadic decision-making or by chance but by a well-developed plan.

According to Singh, Kryscynski, Li, and Gopal (2015), organizations through collaborative networks have access to what is called "combinatory knowledge." Two minds are better than one, as the saying goes. The day of making decisions behind closed doors or trying to solve real and complex problems in schools in a vacuum is, at last, over.

Through professional leadership networks, school superintendents have an excellent opportunity to help the district to access a vast treasure trove of strategies, supports, resources, and information that can help move the district forward and help the district to refocus on what matters the most—the success of ALL students. The complexities that school superintendents face today should be approached with a clear understanding of the gravity and the competing forces that are involved in serving all of our kids.

Start with a basic understanding of professional leadership networks and collaboration and roll up your sleeves. According to Feiock, Lee, and Park (2012), networks and collaboration are by-products of each other. As networks form, the result is collaboration. As collaboration begins to take place, new networks form or existing networks are strengthened. Not only is it acceptable to collaborate and network, but the expectation must also be to effectively communicate in the district that collaboration is vision critical.

Superintendents can strengthen the expectation by embracing what is common in most organizations, and that is found in the belonging feeling of collaboration. According to Battiston, Iacovacci, Nicosia, Bianconi, and Latora (2016), collaboration leads to a group focus on common goals. Just as Fortune 500 collaborate out of the necessity to remain competitive in a competitive global market, school districts must collaborate to stay relevant in a growing competitive educational market.

Collaboration, through internal and external networks, inspires exploration, risk-taking, and innovation, something that all school districts would benefit from today. School districts remain too rigid and fail to recognize the need for more flexibility and innovation when it comes to creating the best-quality education possible for ALL students. The rigidity of school district constructs have become the silent death of many school districts.

When school districts fail to understand the necessity of being flexible in today's highly competitive K-12 market, schools start a downward spiral. Networking and collaboration have helped many superintendents and other system leaders to recognize that without empowerment, the district, as an organization, is destined to become isolated, leading to stagnant growth or, even worse, failure.

The assumption that collaboration is an automatic by-product of professional leadership networks is not factual. In fact, there are key components that must be present in professional leadership networks for collaboration to happen. First and foremost, there must be a certain level of trust we have mentioned in earlier chapters among those actors who engage in networks. Mischen (2015) argues that network success is a result of the leader having social capital and capacity.

In relation to the superintendency, this means that the superintendent is respected by his or her peers, transparent with stakeholders, accessible, culturally responsive, and socially adept. But to expand the basics of collaboration and professional leadership networks, shared goals, trust, existing structures (network processes and practices), and a willingness to be innovative must exist.

Superintendents who are open to listening understand that collaboration is critical to their jobs. We cannot stress enough the importance of trust and the ability of the network to create a new now that is modeled by the superintendent and school system leaders.

According to Willem and Lucidarme (2013), trust and network flexibility are often found to impede the overall success of the professional leadership network. When superintendents see that they can work to ensure connection, then collaboration and network flexibility go hand and hand. In addition, professional leadership networks must adapt to the diverse and changing needs of a continually changing superintendency. The key is that the superintendent engage in the development of network processes that engage a cross section of stakeholders who can sustain relationships during transition and also clearly communicate changes as they occur, if any, in regard to goals, needs, supports, and so on.

PAUSING FOR TECHNOLOGY: PRACTICAL ADVICE

Take a Step with a Digital Footprint

Just knowing that Twitter publishes 50 million tweets a day worldwide should suggest the tech power of a collective collaborative community of social media users. Think of Maslow. Recognize that the center of his pyramid is where belonging in social ways is housed. A major reason people are online and using tech platforms is to belong. Belonging is a stepping stone that leads to a self-actualization—the top of the pyramid. Research suggests that belonging even in the most personal sense, belonging through commitment, is becoming more tech driven. Two out of 10 marriages today are by those who meet online!

Technology offers us the opportunity to cast a wide net into the places where we want to belong. Taking the previous idea of being "Like Me" into the hunt for collaborators internally and externally is made so much easier these days through unifying platforms. The Meetup online community isn't a dating service; it is a source of collective data around finding out WHO is interested in topics that we are interested in exploring.

Topics as far ranging as space to learning to play a guitar have group meetings. Need a quick connecting strategy to learn about your stakeholder culture? Have a look at Meetups in your area that are community oriented. Join those whose cultures are part of your school community. Gather data and new networking partners on your feet after you have researched the groups in your community online who are looking to belong—become part of that group. It is empowering to make these connections on the screen that turn to real-time connectivity.

Superintendents can engage in professional leadership networks through their personal professional brand to increase the feeling of belonging online. Your presence on digital and social channels is a way to acquire and develop the skills needed to empower others as you show your authentic self. Recognize that collaboration always leads to empowerment. Too often, organizations are restricted, confined to cubicles, because of the leader's unwillingness to collaborate or a lack of understanding about the importance of collaboration.

For those who may be more introverted leaders, tech connections may offer you a strategy and safety in increased belonging. You may want to feel more in control of your narrative. If you do have a go at creating and content your own content, a platform like Catcat.com, described in chapter 9, is a place where you can find content in a friendly, personal course like presentation by experts, and YOU can become that expert should you want to belong to the community! It helps leaders to have a "path" of short posts that explains their ongoing vision one—that is done in a way that isn't your school strategic plan style but of a series of relevant topics that help you to advance your brand and to make welcoming connections internally and externally.

Keep a pace. Join groups on LinkedIn, once you have built up your profile as a way for technology to turn your network into a powerful force. Make sure you have a complete profile as you seek belonging in technology. A true picture and a short statement of your personal professional brand, as well as a list of your accomplishments, are necessary for your digital footprint to be seen as authentic. Study the profiles of those you wish to connect with, and see how they present themselves to the collaborative community.

There are numerous opportunities for superintendents who lack an understanding of networking or collaboration through technology. Think about the possibilities of working with collaborating with other superintendents online in Skype conversations, in Zoom meetings, or through Twitter chats to identify key strategies that encourage stakeholders to participate in the professional leadership networks you are building. YouTube videos on key topics can help you learn about collaboration and making connections online that are made by master networkers. The answer is at your fingertips.

Two "edge-dwelling" leaders, thanks to their press buzz and the power of Google Alerts, emerge to demonstrate how tech-savvy leadership results in connectivity that benefits a community. Meet Nicholas Indeglio and Jon Ross, who brand themselves as "The Rock Star Principals" and whose goal is to provide a unique voice in education leadership through a format that is totally "business as unusual" using the pop culture lens of "rock stardom," which gives these two Pennsylvania principals the freedom to showcase the good news around their profession as public school principals and to position challenges in a fresh light. In their one-word brand they provide a VOICE to inspire more than 100,000 unique downloads from their loyal podcast listeners, many of whom are isolated in their positions. Powered by the belief that "you can't change the world from the sidelines," their message is a model for readers. From a quantitative view, they know their message is heard through their show's data and by their 30,000 legitimate Twitter followers who connect with them on @RckStrPrincipal. Their data shows, *Our population wants a voice and wants collegiality and a sense of belonging.*

Okay, so we all can't be rock stars, who fill a room to capacity at national leadership conferences. The message is find your unique brand value we presented in chapter 5. If the superintendent is not comfortable with being the change agent when it comes to collaboration, then empower others who can through their online behavior. Let them be the "buddy change agents" for your mission and empower them to be lead collaborators. When others recognize the power of networks, they are enlightened. In today's networking strategy a connection to the world online is fuel for belonging. Make sure to check out Judy Wilson's appendix for a more complete discussion of how to create yourself as a connected leader through the top social media platforms!

Why are collaboration and networks important in organizations today? Networking to collaborate is critical to the overall organizational effectiveness and long-term sustainability. Thomas, St. (2015, February 8). The value in building networks [Blog Post]. Retrieved from http://www.collaborationforimpact.com/the-value-in-building-networks/. Rowena suggests that networks provide the means to strengthen collaboration. Learn the "Value of Building Networks" by viewing Thomas' (2015) blog by accessing the QR code below.

Superintendents can also develop critical, diverse partnerships that can lead to the sense of belonging and empowerment of others. As school leaders engage in various and relevant networks, they will naturally help other system leaders to develop confidence to empower others to be leaders in the district—through modeling the expectation to collaborate, network, and create systems that engage stakeholders in the district. By encouraging others to engage in networks, they can acquire the skills, resources, and supports needed to be change agents in the transformation of the district.

One of the most important things that superintendents can do is to reflect regularly on their growth and role as a leader in real time and in tech time—online. Before leaders can empower others, they must be empowered to lead themselves. Get rid of the fear of transparency. It's a time of openness that the Internet and social media have powered. Set goals. Reflecting on your growth as a leader regularly can help you assess the gaps in your online profile and performance. Regular reflection also helps identify new ways to expand collaboration.

Superintendents seek these new connecting opportunities with new energy. The idea that networks do not need to be "fine-tuned" every now and then is inaccurate, so use that energy to keep current. Professional leadership networks, just like wired-computer networks, must be updated and checked regularly; professional leadership networks must also be updated. Collaboration is an excellent way to maintain an existing network, while also forming new networks.

School districts face the challenge in an urgency to change their views toward making external partnerships in an information-driven world. For far too long, collaboration among colleagues, partners, or outside stakeholders has been sporadic or nonexistent in school districts across the nation. Collaboration is a driving force in all organizations and can help transform an American icon—our public school districts. Use your growing understanding of digital and social networks to keep pace and then to create your own power.

SETTING A PACE: LEADING AS SUPERINTENDENT

Patience. Persistence. Presence.

Many innovations are the result of thousands of small actions that build up over time. Networking is like that for leaders. The good news is that we are in a time of belonging, a time when despite the isolation of a world of screens, we see human connectivity growing through online and offline behavior. Look for places where you can create the small moments of innovation for connection and becoming in small moments.

Lead with a conversation of belonging in a world that is quickly changing. Have conversations around handling the challenges. Bring thought leaders like leadership consultant and future-forward speaker and writer Heather E. McGowan into your network, via LinkedIn videos and slide shares, to keep you focused on sharing current, trending complex topics with laser focus with your professional learning network.

Talking about the future is tough, but with Heather's three As, the interlocking factors are transforming work for our students: atomization, automation, and augmentation; you can model clear thinking for your learning organization and give leadership value through sharing her content. Be patient and keep going. Superintendents and other school system leaders now realize that they cannot lead a 21st-century school district alone.

Others are willing to step up to the plate and lead, either out front or behind the scenes—in person or on screens. District leaders benefit by a focus on creating opportunities that empower others to lead. Talk at this point in the school districts is not only cheap but also counterproductive. In this digital time, talk is democratized for learning and networking. Take action to empower yourself and others.

Superintendents cannot just talk about empowerment. They can model how to engage, encourage, and empower stakeholders to be part of leading the school district. As discussed earlier, internal professional networks provide an excellent means of building teacher leadership, student leadership, and principal leadership, not to overlook parent and community leadership. Each leadership stakeholder must be part of moving the school district forward and transforming the educational process today. Internal networks are the conduit to placing each empowered individual in position to be transformative at the right place and time.

When school superintendents engage in professional learning, they acquire and develop skills necessary to lead effectively. Professional leadership networks are opportunities for collaborative professional learning for superintendents that empower them to be more strategic, practical, and empowering. Empowerment in an organization doesn't just happen but instead requires ongoing professional learning, collaboration, and a true sense of direction.

When superintendents face obstacles, if they are active in a professional leadership network, they have an immediate support system that can help them to work the problem. They have their own virtual team built from relationships with other district leaders who can offer strategies, suggestions, feedback, and words of encouragement.

Becoming an empowered leader is not easy. It takes work. When effective, it is transformative. It is the most beneficial outcome, and it is always important to remember that your professional networking behavior is directly linked to increased student achievement. Remember, the trickle-down theory works when applied to student achievement. Identify and participate in change in the future of schools through the empowerment of growing networks.

SPOTLIGHTING BUSINESS ACUMEN: PRIVATE SECTOR APPLICATION

Limitless Networking

—John M. Stanley, City Manager, Au Gres Michigan

As I reflect on my young professional career and the network I've created thus far, I find that it's not about taking the path of least resistance but breaking down the walls that create perceived barriers causing resistance on our respective paths. This allows for a networking path that is much wider and much more effective.

I first really discovered the power of networking when I was 23 years old. A year earlier, I made an extremely tough choice to leave law school and jump into the experiential marketing field a year later. It wasn't a planned path but a path created due to a network. In this case, the strength of my network consisted of my best friend who was already with the agency I went to work for.

This agency was one of the largest in Michigan, and I came from one of the smallest cities in the state. That said, a network that started naturally years in advance created an opportunity that put me in my first career of marketing that went on for seven years. This profession opened up long-lasting relationships. Do not underestimate the power of a network that consists initially of your closest friends or the size of the area that you called home.

I left experiential marketing in 2012 in order to return home and build my real estate career with my father, who owns the business. During this time, I continued to build my network through constant contact with every person I worked with, trade associations, local chamber of commerce, and so on. A strong network is created through a mantra similar to sales: treat persons as they are the top priority, regardless of how much they spend and, in the case of a network contact, how far their reach is.

Never assume a new contact you make has a limited network reach: always assume it's limitless. In real estate, the most nominal closing can always turn into the most lucrative. Treat your network as such. Moving forward, I decided in 2014 to continue enhancing and expanding my career along with my professional network, by accepting a position as city manager of my hometown, where I was presently working in the real estate field.

This opportunity created a new tentacle of contacts but, in my opinion, one of my most strongest opportunities was by creating a dynamic partnership with our local school district superintendent Jeffrey Collier. We took on a project of a community podcast, now called Huron Forward. This podcast initially was a celebration of our expanded community along with connecting relevant topics back to the area.

We have been able to expand our professional networks through Huron Forward by embracing the power of digital technology and marketing. Our guest list became multidimensional and spanned nationwide, with international guests in our upcoming season. Huron Forward has allowed us to intertwine the importance of community, business, and education into one symbiotic body. In summary, I have found a strong network is created by not ruling out the obvious and embracing the unexpected.

PIVOTING POINTERS FOR CHAPTER 8

- Empowerment does not weaken leadership in the district; instead, it strengthens the leadership capacity in the district.
- Professional leadership networks are empowering as superintendents, other district leaders, and staff members can access simple, strategic, and relevant professional learning opportunities.
- Superintendents, when they are active in professional leadership networks, can utilize to grow professionally, while also growing the district as an organization.
- No matter the size, professional leadership networks can be empowering. Professional leadership networks do not need to be sophisticated to be empowering; in fact, the simpler, the better, as sophistication often leads to confusion and disengagement.
- Professional leadership networks in real time and online provide participants key learning opportunities that are empowering—as those who actively engage in collaboration acquire critical skills, strategies, and resources that are empowering the individual and the organization that they represent.

Chapter 9

MOBILIZING: Claiming Your Social and Digital Leadership Networking Presence

Who you will someday be, you are now becoming.
If you're going to be anything, be social!

—Judith Wilson, MEd

CONNECTED EDUCATOR'S VIGNETTE

As school leaders, we are always learning, growing, and evolving. As a result, each and every school year we change. To prove it to yourself, glance back to the beginning of your career as an educator. You won't even see a glimmer of the person you are today. The reason is you don't act the same, talk the same, and even look the same. Just check out your arms. It's a connected world. After all these years, your arms have grown so long, they've stretched so far, and they reach so wide. So exactly what has happened to you? Social media happened. That's what.

On the pages that follow, I attempt to break down the top social media platforms for you using three significant questions: "What's it about?" "What does it mean?" and "Why should you care?" I want you to care—or you won't make the move.

Now, use those long arms and reach in for a brand new understanding of social media and a new or renewed *awakening* of your senses to the sights, sounds, and feel of our 21st-century digital, social, and camera culture. Be aware of the power that social media packs and how it can help you transition to *becoming* a digital *edu*preneur, well equipped with a social media strategy that showcases your school's unique brand value and the *branding* that distinguishes you.

The results will be visible in improved school culture, performance, and resources. Let this new and renewed awareness of social media belay your fears of stepping up, of trying things differently in a way that is both purposeful and successful. Be prepared for the *deepening* of your networking skills as you grow your PLN (professional learning network). Let's face it; you have all the technology you need to get started right in your pocket. The *reaching* is real. You've got the whole world in your hands. Reach. Position yourself. Nothing can compare to the learning that comes from this engaged experience and the comfort of *belonging*. Embrace a personal professional challenge. It's time to *mobilize*.

Do it. Be social. Take it on personally today. I'm excited for you. Good luck!

SETTING THE PACE: LEADING AS SUPERINTENDENT

Socializing 101

THE CONNECTED LEADER'S GUIDE TO SOCIAL MEDIA

Twitter

What Is It?

- It's an online news and social networking platform.
- It's about communicating in messages known as "tweets."
- It's about initiating, growing connections, networking, conversation, brand building, researching, and learning.
- It's about 280 characters or less.

What Does It Mean?

- The brevity and conciseness of the message means you can skim through your news feed and get the general idea of what's trending and what's happening.
- It means registered users can share updates, press releases, events, launches, news, and all kinds of information. You can even do video go "live." But don't use it solely for that. Twitter is a social platform. So be social!
- It means you can start a conversation, ask for advice, foster engagement, and connect with friends and other fascinating people. It means you can stay up to date on all kinds of things that interest you.

- It means tweets are publicly visible by default, but senders can restrict message delivery to just their followers.
- As a social network, Twitter revolves around the principle of followers. When you choose to follow another Twitter user, that user's tweets appear on your main Twitter page.
- It means you should get started and get social. Create an account, start following others, and create content for yourself. Learn the lingo—# (hashtag), PLN (professional learning network), RT (retweet), and DM (direct message).
- It means you can join a Twitter chat. Have a public conversation at a set time with like-minded individuals around a unique hashtag. The hashtag allows you to follow and participate in the discussion. Twitter chats are usually on specific topics to regularly connect people with like interests.
- Once you're on Twitter, it means you are open for conversation. It means you can make all the positives so loud that the negatives are almost impossible to hear. Once you're on, you'll regret having waited so long.

Why Should You Care?

- Because your parents, student, staff, and community are on. Listen to what they're saying. Take it a step further and use your presence as an opportunity to be a social-media role model for your digital natives—your students.
- Because your PLN is priceless. Once you establish who they are, they become your go-to for collaborating, learning, and reflecting on your leadership. Discover new influencers, competitors, and opinions, and join in conversations.
- Because your biggest fear is that people are talking about you or your school district. What if they are and you don't know anything about what they're saying? Twitter is an accessible way for people to contact you and for you to contact them.

Facebook

What Is It?

- Facebook is about social networking. It is a platform where users can post comments and share photographs and links to news or other interesting content on the web. Users can play games, chat live, and stream live video.
- It's about choice. Facebook allows you to maintain a friends list, which can be modified as you choose. Choose your privacy settings to customize who can see content on your profile.
- It's about sharing content that can be made accessible to the public, or it can be shared only among your select group of friends or family, or with a single person.

- It's about the lens. Facebook allows you to upload photos and maintain photo albums that can be shared with your friends.
- It's about supporting interactive online chats and the ability to comment on your friend's "wall" or profile page; in order to keep in touch, share information or just say "hi."
- It's about supporting group pages, fan pages, and business pages that let businesses use Facebook as a means for social media marketing—branding.
- It's about #hashtags. Hashtags help people easily find out what others are saying about a given topic and to participate in public conversations. Find out who is talking and what they are saying by clicking on a hashtag or searching. Are they talking about you, your school, your district, your policies, procedures, events? Yes. You definitely want to get in on that.
- It's about Facebook Messenger, which is the second most popular messaging app behind WhatsApp. People use Facebook individually, joining or setting up groups.

What Does It Mean?

- It means the time is now for you to unleash the power of your story and move beyond the status quo.
- It means Facebook can take you where you don't necessarily want to go but ought to be—building an engaged community where you cocreate and co-own the future together.
- It means you live in a competitive, digitized world that is built on transparency.
- It means that you can decide whether to customize your page for your personal use or business/school/district use. For example, if you're looking to grow your own professional learning network, then sharing articles and doing Q&As can be beneficial in extending your reach.
- It means that you can use Facebook to listen to the voices of the students, the parents, the staff, and community and respond to them in order to show caring about the brand of the school and how it is maintained.

Why Should You Care?

- Because Facebook is too big for you to ignore. Worldwide, as of March 2018, 1.45 billion people on average log onto Facebook every day. There are over 2.20 billion monthly active Facebook users for the first quarter of 2018 (*Source*: Facebook April 25, 2018). Approximately five new profiles are created every second.
- Because Facebook is your small portion of personal real estate on the Internet where you get to make the choices about whom you communicate with, be it your school families, staff, students, your community, or the whole wide world. Yes, the whole wide world. You choose the settings.

- Because you'll stay in the know by getting current and personalized news and updates from your Facebook "friends" as well as updates from brands, blogs, and public figures. All of these are delivered to you via your news feed.
- Because we live in a "camera culture" that daily creates new ways to capture and share information. Billions of people are making the invisible become visible by posting and sharing photos and live videos. Photo uploads to Facebook total 300 million per day (*Source*: Gizmodo), and you, your students, your staff, and your community are in them.
- Because you'll tear down school walls and show the world all the great things you are doing just by uploading and sharing pictures or by going live. You'll focus on communicating content and you'll control the narrative.
- Because people are definitely talking about you, your school, your district, your policies, procedures, events, and more. You want to definitely get in on the conversations so you can have some control over the message.

Instagram

What Is It?

- Instagram is about sharing your story via the app by posting simple photos and videos. It is used by millions of people across the globe. It has become more than about being a social platform for users to share their experiences with family and friends.
- It's about just anyone using Instagram to create visual narratives about what makes them different from everything else that's out there.
- It's about being a complete powerhouse among rival social networks. And if you think anything different, you may want to reconsider. Take a look at how some of the top CEOs like John Legere of T-Mobile are using it to build brand.
- It's about *showing* how great your school district is rather than always just *talking* about how great it is. The photo editing is really cool. You can upload a photo and edit it in many ways. By adding a filter, cropping your image, or even just changing the brightness of a video, the editing options help you showcase your schools in interesting and artistic ways. Many users choose to link their Instagram with their other social media platforms solely because of the editing tools.

What Does It Mean?

- It means we are watching Instagram grow to become a complete powerhouse among rival social networks.
- It means you should be using Instagram to build your school brand. If you're thinking anything different, you may want to reconsider.

- It means there's strength in numbers. Instagram stats show that as of March 2018 there are currently more than 800 million monthly active users, and many experts believe it will reach a billion very soon. That's more than double the monthly active users of Twitter and over three times as many users on WhatsApp and Facebook Messenger. That's strong evidence that you can use Instagram to build your school brand.
- It means you can leverage the power of Instagram to promote your school brand just by an Instagram post each day. It will keep your community connected to what you deem as important for brand building.
- It means you are able to utilize many hashtags that will align your post to what is relevant, meaningful, and engaging.
- It means even if you are fearful of a digital footprint, there's something here for you—the Instagram Story. It lasts for a mere 24 hours, and it can include as many posts as you like. You can even save your story if you decide you don't want it to disappear.
- It means we need to repeat this to you—it's a "camera culture." A picture speaks a thousand words.

Why Should You Care?

- Because if you don't have a free Instagram account, you should be suffering from an acute case of #fomo. Remember, they *are* talking about you. Experts predict that Instagram could reach 200 billion active monthly users by the end of 2018. This means your school community is counted in the number of active users. The first step in getting somewhere is to decide you're not going to stay where you are.
- Because Instagram is a perfect place to store all your content, it will drive your visitors back to your school/district website.
- Because you thought your blog content had to reside on your "blog" page. By combining your blog copy with Instagram captions and making it pop with an inviting image, you create every blogger's dream. Why? Because Instagram is fun! It's also more casual and less scripted than a blog, and your school community is spending time there instead of on Facebook and blog pages.

LinkedIn

What Is It?

- LinkedIn is a social networking platform for professionals like you who want their visibility to extend far beyond the school community.
- It means you create your profile designed to look almost like very detailed resumes, with sections for education, work experience, volunteer work,

certifications, awards, and all kinds of other relevant, work-related information.
- It means you create your headline, an underused yet important element of your LinkedIn profile. Your headline should show your uniqueness and the value of your accomplishments.
- It means you should make the most out of the group feature, which most people ignore when they first join, so you can instantly expand your PLN. There are quite a few well-populated groups for educators just like you.
- It means you can also form your own group to connect, brainstorm, and discuss. The sky's the limit.

What Does It Mean?

- It's about promoting yourself and your position by making connections with other professionals.
- It's about managing current connections and making new ones by interacting in discussions with individuals or groups, posting job openings, applying for jobs, posting articles you wrote, or perhaps sharing articles with others.
- It's about developing yourself as a content producer and publisher.
- It's about using your own voice in a short one-minute LinkedIn message to stay connected.
- It's about a platform for those like you who want to advance their careers and make connections. Showcase uniqueness and any other talents and interests you have. It's a place to showcase what makes you remarkable, worth making a remark about.
- It's about joining those who use LinkedIn to connect with a professional community from around the world and pick the brains of experts in the field.

Why Should You Care?

- Because LinkedIn is the best way for a school administrator to up his or her professional game on the Internet.
- Because LinkedIn combines the best aspects of Twitter and Facebook to create an online space for networking and brainstorming with a global cohort that is professional and purposeful.
- Because LinkedIn makes the world even smaller. Have you ever gone to a conference or read a book or article and wished you could meet the amazing speaker or author? Well, LinkedIn makes that possible.
- Because it's one thing for you to say you are a caring, compassionate school leader but it's much more momentous when it comes from someone else. *Recommendations* give a LinkedIn profile increased dimension. Through

LinkedIn, you can ask former or current colleagues, classmates, or collaborators for a recommendation. You can also write a testimonial for any person you are connected to through LinkedIn.
- Because as a school administrator you should commit maintaining at least one *strictly professional* online channel and LinkedIn is an excellent choice.

WhatsApp

What Is It?

- WhatsApp Messenger is a FREE mobile messaging app available for iPhone and other smartphones.
- WhatsApp uses your phone's Internet connection to let you message and call friends and family. Switch from SMS to WhatsApp to send and receive messages, calls, photos, videos, and voice messages.
- It means the app can facilitate one-to-one or group messaging and content sharing.
- It means the app can essentially mesh together traditional messaging services, social media, and your phone for a fully immersive messaging platform.
- It means WhatsApp provides an easy and effective messaging system within teams that is simple and productive.

What Does It Mean?

- It's about more than texting and sharing photos one to one. It's about establishing a group PLN after a conference, PD, a training, or a meeting of key stakeholders. Invite them to a WhatsApp group! It will enhance and promote leadership conversations and help enhance networking among participants, well after they've returned to their school sites.
- It's about establishing norms for your group conversation, like *it should not be used for personal or other purposes*; and *everyone is encouraged to participate in the discussions/reflections.*
- It's about using the app to transfer learning within your group and to remind and encourage each other to reach a goal. Maybe it even creates a little healthy peer pressure.
- It's about using the app as an efficient way to follow up with workshop participants post training. It's a way to help participants remember the goals they had set for themselves and to remind them of the content of the training.

Why Should You Care?

- Because likeminded school leaders are already using the WhatsApp platform in their professional learning community. Teams of educators armed with smartphones, the WhatsApp application, and Wi-Fi can all receive the

Mobilizing 143

same message at the same time and are able to respond. They are sending individual and group messages anywhere in the world. They are sending and receiving photos, videos, recordings, and Word documents.
- Because those holding group conversations using WhatsApp are saying it motivates the participants to put into action what they had learned during trainings, professional developments, book study, conferences, and so on.
- Because follow-up after professional gatherings is often hard to do but not with this app. WhatsApp helps participants to remember what they have seen in a training, PD, or at a conference and remember to apply it.
- Because it's a brilliant and helpful way to use an app to see what colleagues are doing in their schools, take ideas, and get motivated by what others do. When you see other schools making changes, it motivates you to want to do the same. If they can do it, why can't you? A little encouragement from a group goes a long way, too.
- Because it makes perfect sense. It's an app that many colleagues already know how to use; it is free, readily accessible, and available.

Snapchat

What Is It?

- Snapchat is a wildly popular and fun mobile app. It is both a messaging platform and a social network.
- It allows you to chat with one or multiple friends at once, send photos and/or 60-second videos, send private messages, and make voice and video calls.
- It is temporary, and everything posted will self-destruct in 24 hours. Poof! Gone! But beware, anyone can screenshot and immortalize your snaps.
- It lets you send "Stories." Stories are a feed of the images recently posted that can be watched by anyone who follows you, similar to Stories on Instagram and Facebook.

What Does It Mean?

- It means designing. Snapchat geofilters. Geofilters are festive sticker-like, graphic overlays for Snaps that can only be accessed in certain locations and change depending on where you are taking your photo or video. They dress up your snap with pretty graphics to stamp your location. The geofilters I see in New York are different from those you see in Kentucky.
- It means creating photos with free geofilters. They are everywhere in your community already. They are available only within a certain range, approximately 20,000 square feet or more.

- It means branding! You can buy a geofilter with your school mascot/logo. You can change your geofilter to commemorate school events, seasons, and holidays. When students, staff, and visitors take pictures at your school, they will add your geofilter to their photos and videos. And just like that, your school identifiers are shared on a new channel.
- It means dressing up your snaps with bitmojis, emojis, text, and animation.
- It means facial recognition. Snapchat matches your face to animations using computer vision, used more and more in our society. It means you scan your checks and the data is extracted from the lines. It means you can deposit checks with your phone. It is how Facebook knows who's in your photos and how self-driving cars can avoid running over people.

Why Should You Care?

- Because Snapchat is the most important social network for your students. It is reportedly ahead of Instagram, Twitter, or Facebook. Snapchat appeals to your younger mobile users. This statistic presents the number of daily active Snapchat users as of the first quarter of 2018 from Statisa.com. As of the latest reported period, Snapchat had 191 million daily active users worldwide, up from 166 million global daily active users in the corresponding quarter of the previous year.
- Because the power of a story should not come as a surprise to you. In education, you need to be cognizant that you are also marketers. Our product is creating future problem solvers.
- Because Snapchat is a great tool to tell your story. It is one of the few that lets you share content and context in just a few seconds. The app doesn't break up your story and message into bits and pieces across a person's news feed. It provides a continuous stream where you see the development of an idea, activity, or thought from start to finish.
- Because it's a way of blasting out information that students will see. Kids between ages 13 and 22 have a dreadfully low e-mail check and open rate.
- Because it is a way for educators to share out a change of event, breaking news or a demonstration, or cool piece of content to their students on the app that takes up 80 percent of their time.
- Because getting started on Snapchat now will only help you understand how this platform is being used by your school community. Use it so you can understand the major implications for teaching, communication, and sharing. Snapchat is evolving with every month that passes. It's relevant to your school community, and it is here to stay. Are you?

Pinterest

What Is It?

- Pinterest is about a focus on striking visuals and imagery in order to make it the perfect platform for schools, retailers, and lifestyle brands that want to share their most eye-catching content with an engaged and active community. Most users are below 34 years.
- It's about scrapbooking and collecting, only it's an Internet version. It's a place that lets you to find, collect, and organize interesting image-based things that you find on the Internet, find on a website, or put on the website yourself. It does this through a series of user-created categories, called "boards," and a series of visual bookmarks, known as "pins."

What Does It Mean?

- It means you can pin and archive *your* school photos of school events, classroom charts, student work, school supply lists, and school uniforms and find ideas for fundraising events. Search around and see what other schools are pinning on their boards.
- It means you can find photos, drawings, videos, animations, and video links for leadership quotes, teacher lessons, observation protocols, coaching and team-building activities, makerspace ideas, STEM activities, professional development ideas, and unique classroom configurations and even find the latest discussion guides for Ted Talks for Aspiring Student Leaders and more!

Why Should You Care?

- Because there are about 12 million users in the United States. It's among the most popular social networks in the United States in terms of traffic.
- Because it's growing in popularity. Just ask around your school community. They'll tell you they are spending a lot of time here, on average of 98 minutes per month.
- Because Pinterest members are using it to associate with retailers or brands with which they identify and you can be using it to promote your school/district brand and increase the number of people who identify with your school brand.
- Because it's about staying relevant. Pinterest members say they use it to keep up with the latest trends and brands. The worst thing about being left out is knowing you weren't even a simple thought on any of their minds after the school day ended. Your school brand needs to show up. No?

Catcat

What Is It?

- Catcat is a free learning destination that encourages anyone to curate, share, discover, and consume information related to their individual passions or areas of expertise.
- Its ultimate goal is to democratize learning and help people acquire the skills they need to become more successful at work and in life. Basically, it wants to change the way people learn.
- It is promoting its strong belief that all the information needed to learn a subject already exists online and people like us are creating more awesome content every day. But every day learning is still not right. They want to change that. Catcat doesn't want us to be forced into learning by paying higher education organizations for a degree or be dictated to as to what we find valuable or spend too much time sifting through and eliminating content.

What Does It Mean?

- It means saying the name—Catcat. You won't forget it.
- It means striving to empower anyone to leverage his or her expertise and passion to identify, organize, and share the best of the bite-size information that is already freely available online.
- It means growing a community of highly engaged curators and learners that is changing the way the world learns.
- It means building a better way for people all over the world to access the best of the free content that is already available on the Web.

Why Should You Care?

- Because it's about the way we learn and the way we consume information and how we connect these to job performance, career development, and overall happiness. And we are in the business of educating today's youth and preparing them for college and careers while nurturing their social-emotional health. We are a perfect match.

MENTION: MISTAKES? I'VE MADE A FEW. TOO FEW TO "MENTION"

Are you monitoring online *mentions* in conversations? It's a big mistake not to. Your school's community is huge. It includes its past, present, and future students; parents and families of those students; fans of your clubs and teams;

its local community; and really just about anyone. Social media monitoring tools measure the "social value" of your school brand and provide important traffic insights you can use to improve your decisions. Whether you want to be a social listener by observing quietly, learning about your community and what they are looking for, responding to your critics, or just engaging in conversation, *you need to know what your people are saying about you.*

IN CLOSING

There are many tools out there to help you monitor your school brand by tracking *mentions* on social media and blogs. Find one you like to monitor the names of your schools, sports teams, faculty, location, and even hashtags. They can help you find everything you need to know. And listening should always be at the top of your social media priorities even before you create your social media strategy.

Here are just a few digital tools:

Socialmention
Mention
Hootsuite
Google Alerts
Tweetdeck
Hashtrackin
Feedly

Conclusion

> What I've learned over a lifetime of sailing across the world is that all waves eventually take you to the shore.
>
> —Anonymous

In the pages of *ConnectED Leaders* we have presented seven unifying leadership concepts: *awakening, becoming, branding, deepening, reaching, belonging,* and *mobilizing*. As in the preceding quotes, these concepts are the shores. They are the powerful, big ideas, separated by the waves, standing like continents with welcoming shores and unique landscapes. These continents can be visited by travelers who can engage in and create experiences.

They are connected by the journey of sailing. At the end of the book, we now ask you about your journey. How many big ideas will you take on? How many shores you choose to connect with is up to you. We hope you travel. We want you to spend purposeful time alone or with a crew on the sea of organizational change as you venture forward. We invite you into this metaphor hoping it will create connection for you as you captain your ship and embark on a *connectED* journey.

In the chapters of *ConnectED Leaders*, we advanced thinking supported by research, and we suggested strategies and tools. We've presented stories. We've shared powerful testimonials to convince you of the need to become networked and *connectED*. Our reasoning began with superintendents *awakening* to the fact that the school landscape is changing rapidly. Creating a new model superintendency has a sense of urgency about it.

With this rapid change in public education, superintendents must see their leadership stance as a leader in continuous learning, always *becoming*. One of the first elements in presenting a new, open model of leadership is found in *branding*. With an authentic, personal professional brand, a leader can look to *deepening* communication in the internal organizational system to inspire more collaborative and networked school culture.

To remain a relevant and critical player, you must journey outside to the unlimited opportunities beyond the educational organization, expanding the story of the school, taking the leadership brand to other "cross-industry" shores, and *reaching* for connection that can power school success in new ways. Through hard work in simple and complex situations, a new culture of *belonging* can emerge that sustains a "crew" on the continuous journey and allows the comfort of traveling to other communities, near and far, online and in real time, to connect in new ways.

Finally, *mobilizing* is a means to start your journey using tools as diverse as the people you will meet and connect with. Collaborative power grows as professional leadership networks bring opportunities for superintendents as captains, to access resources, supports, and critical talent to ignite change within their organization.

Like the sailor's voice in the metaphor, superintendents must welcome the journey across the waves, large and small. Creating change as an open leader means embracing the known and unknown on the charted and uncharted waters, leading by being continually informed, connected, and networked. Unlike any time before in public education, collaboration is critical. The rate of change has never been as accelerated, and it's quickening thanks to artificial intelligence, augmented reality, and virtual reality.

Failure to adapt from isolated to collaborative positioning will cause many leaders to be left behind on the shores in their school districts, their home ports, where they risk through isolation the chance to grow themselves, but most important, they fail to produce prepared members of the next generation. Our students must be agile, open, and connected to their learning if they are to keep pace as adults in a world made new almost every day by this rapid change, by new economies, new politics, new ideology, new technology, new media, and many more new constructs that continue to shape their lives. As we close *ConnectED Leaders*, we encourage superintendents to care, embrace collaboration, network, and lead as the collaborative captains journeying to the future.

There is a saying in the south the "good Lord works in mysterious ways and always at the right time." Every person you meet in life and as a leader is meant to be. Embrace the opportunity, follow the network, live, and grow. Never forget that ALL great leaders are surrounded by a team, an internal or external network of "critical friends."

Afterword

I learned very early in my career that our colleagues are our best resources, our best support, and, in fact, sometimes our best friends. On my first day in my second superintendency, as a new superintendent in New York, my neighbor called me to wish me well and to take me out to lunch. Nearly 27 years later I am still in touch with and grateful to Mike Osnato. I've passed forward that welcome to others.

I also deeply believe that we must be critical friends to one another. I want my colleagues to succeed and will be critical not only in terms of being candid, but also being there for them in those critical times of need. My career has been dependent on learning from and connecting to other superintendents. In fact, every superintendency I held I was intentional in meeting the superintendents in that region. For example, when I was superintendent in Cherry Hill, New Jersey, we launched the Southern Jersey Standards Consortium. I also met with colleagues from across the state to read and learn, under the gentle guidance of Bena Kallick.

In 2015 I was honored to join AASA, The School Superintendents Association, to expand this work to a national level. During my time as associate executive director for Leadership Services we have added more than 30 professional development programs for our members; we have more than 2,000 district leaders who have engaged with AASA on a continued basis through these programs. I am deeply moved when we visit districts and see changes that reflect the conversations and learning going on in our networks.

The book captures so well what many of us see as part of our commitment to each other and to the students and communities we service. It reflects the commitment that superintendents can make to become leaders in their personal and professional development. It outlines seven strategies for educational leaders to use: **Awakening**, recognizing the context for creating new networks; **Becoming**, innovating and disrupting beyond the traditional ivory tower; **Branding**, designing the image, promise, and result of a leadership networking brand; **Deepening**, inspiring internal networks for community growth; **Reaching**, discovering connectivity in building external networks; **Belonging**, supporting systems and frameworks that sustain a networking strategy; and **Mobilizing**, claiming your social and digital leadership networking presence. The seven strategies outlined provide a framework for where to start on this journey and how to get the most out of it. Personal and professional development is both necessary and important.

Some see the superintendency as "the loneliest job." We may be the only person in our role in a community, but the rewards and opportunities are many. The challenges are daunting, yet we know that there are others in the next town or the next state or across the country who want to learn and grow with you. Because public education is the means by which we sustain our democracy, the importance and success of our work cannot be understated. Nor can we forget for a second that learning is at our core, for all of us. *ConnectED Leaders* reminds each of us that to improve as a profession, we must first improve as professionals.

Morton Sherman, EdD, Associate Executive Director,
AASA, The School Superintendents Association

ConnectED Advice for Your Journey

Social Media, Leadership, and the Superintendent

Dr. Diane Hatchett, Superintendent
Berea Community Schools, Kentucky

In the world that we live in today, communication is key. One of the best and most efficient modes of communication is the Internet. Social media allows for real-time, anytime communication. As a superintendent you have to get your message out there in as many ways as possible. We live in a technological society. Our students are digital natives; many parents, particularly millennials, communicate strictly through their cell phone. In order to capture the attention of stakeholders, we must be able to speak the language of and engage the listener or, in this case, the receiver of information.

Leaders lead by example. I am a strong proponent of the use of social media. I try to set a personal example of what I expect of others. Being on social media allows parents, teachers, students, and the community at large to hear the message the way I want it presented. It builds trust and credibility; it leaves you vulnerable, which makes you for lack of a better word, real. People are able to see what you as a superintendent value and subscribe to directly, up close and personal via social media. Social media exposes you to a wide audience. It provides an invitation and an opportunity to showcase and tell the story of the district.

Strong schools and strong communities go hand in hand. There are so many great things going on at Berea Community Schools. Social media allows me to give a shout-out to my students, parents, faculty, staff, and the community at large. I am always searching for opportunities to get the word out with vivid details about our accomplishments both great and small.

Superintendents must lead the charge in order to facilitate a spirit of community among the stakeholders.

By utilizing social media, I am able to capitalize on new and innovative ways to communicate effectively and efficiently. I enthusiastically share my vision, passion, and beliefs through words, deeds, symbols, photos, and action. The use of social media gives voice to my district's mission and its culture. It is a way to market our brand and model the way whether celebratory or informative.

A picture is worth a thousand words; when I utilize Instagram, LinkedIn, Facebook, and Snapchat, it allows for visual storytelling. It also allows me to keep a digital record or portfolio documenting milestones, events, and successes within the district. I use Twitter to promote reflection, inspire others, and challenge thinking. I can bring matters to life in a matter of a click on the computer. We should always keep learning styles in mind when communicating. Just as people learn differently, they also interact and communicate differently. Some prefer written communication; some prefer text messages, some prefer face-to-face. Social media creates a platform to reach each type of learner who also has different preferences of communication.

Leaders are risk-takers. As a superintendent, communication often must be strategic and planned. You want to get your message out to as many people as possible. As a superintendent, I strive to be purposeful, intentional, creative, and transparent in my communications with others. The use of social media provides a vehicle to get ahead of potential problems, putting out fires before they can spark. Often in the role of superintendent, we need to get a message out as fast as possible; social media allows for things not only to go out quickly and accurately; it can go viral. This is particularly important in times of crisis.

There are so many benefits to utilizing social media. Twitter, LinkedIn, blogs, podcast, and YouTube have time and again served as sources of professional development for superintendents. I have acquired some of my best information through interactions with leading experts in the field and recommendations found on these sites by other superintendents. The personal and professional growth opportunities for dialogue and immediate feedback are incredible.

I have frequently found clips, quotes, pictures, ideas, and information on these sites that have increased my knowledge base on a variety of topics. I do not hesitate to share links, sites, articles, and contacts made with both district school staff and colleagues when applicable for a presentation or research project. Networking is crucial for a superintendent. The more resources we can acquire, the better. Without question, social media opens the doors to a realm of possibilities for superintendents. We can disseminate and receive information that can in a matter of seconds influence a great number of people and in effect change the world in which live.

Perception is reality. I would challenge superintendents to put their best foot forward using social media as a vehicle for visibility, transparency, and communication. It is free, facilitates connections with stakeholders, and creates a unique platform for teaching and learning. Face it folks: we live not only in a global society but in a digital one as well. We can get with the program, look beyond our physical and geographical boundaries, share ideas, learn from others, process feedback, or be left behind. I for one have no plans for my district to be left behind. We will utilize every tool available to us. We are kid driven! We can and will always aim high and dare to be great!

Appendix: AASA Member Blogs

We would be remiss if we did not provide you with a list of superintendents to follow via social media, following Dr. Hatchett's important advice to connect. As we have encouraged you to do throughout our book, we recommend that you become a member of AASA and access the many resources that they provide to new, aspiring, retired superintendents, along with other district leaders. One of the resources that AASA offers, as America's superintendents' "Network Connector," is a list of superintendents to follow.

We provide you a QR code that will link you to AASA's Member Blogs. Many of the superintendents who are listed also have social media profiles that you can access. The members' blogs are influential and filled with content focused on today's education in a view from the field. The superintendents are not only practitioners in the field but also advocates and authors who educate the general public and lend a voice to policy matters through their writings. We would strongly recommend reaching out using the strategies and tools in the text with the superintendents listed to grow your PLN. The superintendents listed are a valued part of the strategic, collaborative, and empowering network of AASA.

Enjoy listening to today's superintendents. Network with the best in the field today at the following linked QR code. Like you, these leaders are looking for "critical friends" in hope that they will become part of their evolving *ConnectED Leaders* network.

A Final Thought: Chief Networker

A superintendent serves as the voice of a school district. The school system leader is also the face of the district and community. A district's ambassador, cheerleader, source of reason, and when times are tough, chief motivator, a superintendent has one of the most difficult jobs in the community as well as the entire nation.

No textbook can prepare a superintendent for the many facets of what the job entails or how to handle specific situations. However, what is becoming more evident in today's educational environment is how valuable networks are to the overall effectiveness of the superintendent and the school district.

Administrators must utilize the many networks that exist. They must opt for collaboration rather than isolation as a tool for professional growth. Collaboration should transcend the geographic boundaries that exist for many superintendents. Think about the vast experience that awaits a superintendent, educational leader and teacher if they access an energized network. Many exist virtually. The tools are limitless. Today, leaders have access to resources and supports like never before.

AASA, The School Superintendents Association, takes pride in serving as a collaborative organization that serves superintendents and other school system leaders through a variety of professional networking opportunities. Superintendents must recognize they are not alone and if they need "critical friends" or "critical partners" to be effective in their jobs, AASA is here to help.

I cannot stress enough how important communication is to joining a network and creating a culture of collaboration. One critical component of networking is communication – using the many digital tools that exist. As I mentioned earlier, superintendents are the voice of the district. How you communicate will open or close networking opportunities for you as a leader and the district as an organization.

As a leader, you and others need to be accessing the many networks that are available. If there isn't a network available, then form one – a sort of "do-it-yourself" project. It may be hard to get a network running, but the rewards would be plentiful.

Work toward accessing networks that are aligned with your goals, needs and aspirations. As the district's CEO, you must lead by example – model how to collaborate and access district, regional and state networks. Conversely, as a leader, if you work in isolation, so too will principals, teachers, and staff members. Silos can develop quickly and are not easily removed once established in an organization.

Your school district must be a culture of collaboration, if you expect the district to be student-centered and focused on the success for ALL students. As superintendent, the more you model collaboration and clearly communicate the expectation, the less likely silos will form. Silos are counterproductive to overall organizational effectiveness, professional growth and student achievement. As superintendent, you need to be leading the charge to create strategic internal and external networks.

Networks are critical to your success – embrace the opportunities that are available.

James Minichello Director,
Communications and Marketing AASA,
The School Superintendents Association

Bibliography

INTRODUCTION

Hill, L., and Lineback, K. (2011, March). The three networks you need. *Harvard Business Review*. Retrieved from https://hbr.org/2011/03/the-three-networks-you-need.html

Perera, A. K. (2014). *Perceptions of females in Virginia regarding the personal and professional factors impacting their career paths to the superintendency* (doctoral dissertation).

Setting the Stage

LANDR. (2018). Creative tools for musicians. Retrieved from https://www.landr.com/en/

Ultromics. (2017). Revolutionising cardiovascular diagnosis. Retrieved from http://www.ultromics.com

CHAPTER 1

Carvill, M. (2018). *Get social: Social media strategies & tactics for leaders*. Great Britain and New York, NY, United States: Kogan Page Limited.

Godin, S. (2014). *What to do when it's your turn (and it's always your turn)*. Seth Godin. United States: The Domino Project.

Ibarra, H. (2008). Networking is vital for successful managers. Insead Knowledge. Retrieved from https://knowledge.insead.edu/leadership-organisations/networking-is-vital-for-successful-managers-2085

Price, D. (2013). [*Open : How we'll work, live and learn in the future*. England]: Crux.

CHAPTER 2

Bailey, D. (2017, July 27). Is the customer really always right? A hotel company invests in its employees first [blog post]. Retrieved from https://www.nist.gov/blogs/blogrige/customer-really-always-right-hotel-company-invests-its-employees-first

Gallo, C. (2018, May 9). Jeff Bezos replaces PowerPoint with narratives in all Amazon presentations—Here's why. *Inc.* Retrieved from https://www.inc.com/carminegallo/jeff-bezos-bans-powerpoint-in-meetings-his-replacement-is-brilliant.html

OECD. (2003). *Networks of innovation: Towards new models for managing schools and systems.* Schooling for Tomorrow. Paris: OECD Publishing. Retrieved from https://doi.org/10.1787/9789264100350-en

Vozza, S. (2015, February 20). Why your company should consider banning email. *Fast Company.* Retrieved from https://www.fastcompany.com/3042541/why-your-company-should-consider-banning-email

CHAPTER 3

Carvill, M. (2018). *Get social: Social media strategy and tactics for leaders.* New York, NY: Kogan Page.

Clark, D. (2015, April). Why public schools are finally getting savvy about marketing. *Forbes* magazine. Retrieved from https://www.forbes.com/sites/dorieclark/2015/04/27/why-public-schools-are-finally-getting-savvy-about-marketing/#119b05437e54

Creasman, B., Bacon, J., and Franklin, D. (2018). *Can every school succeed? Bending constructs of an American icon.* Lanham, MD: Rowman and Littlefield.

Kramer, B. (2014). *There is no B2B or B2C: It's human to human: H2H.* United States: Bryan Kramer & Pure Matter, Inc.

McCreery, J. K., Mazur, L. M., and Rothenberg, L. (2011, January). Exploring the power of social networks and leadership styles during lean program implementation in hospitals. IIE Annual Conference. Proceedings (p. 1), Institute of Industrial and Systems Engineers (IISE).

Networking is vital for successful managers (2007). Insead Knowledge. Retrieved from https://knowledge.insead.edu/leadership-organisations/networking-is-vital-for-successful-managers-2085

Only Best Quotes (2017, May 24). The 95 Best Quotes by George Bernard Shaw [Video file]. Retrieved from https://www.youtube.com/watch?v=CdlK8LkdSb0

Reagans, R., and Zuckerman, E. W. (2001). Networks, diversity, and productivity: The social capital of corporate R & D teams. Organization Science, 12(4), 393–521.

Seifert, T., and Bar-Tal, S. (2017). Participants in a social-professional network foreducators. Journal of Educational Technology, 13(4), 22–37.

Sheninger, E., and Rubin, T. (2017). *BrandED: Tell your story, build relationships and empower learning.* San Francisco, CA: Jossey-Bass.

CHAPTER 4

Davidson, J. R., and Middleton, C. A. (2006). Networking, networking, networking: The role of professional association memberships in mentoring and retention of science librarians. *Science & Technology Libraries,* 27(1/2), 203–224.

Hickman, G. R. (Ed.). (1998). *Leading organizations: Perspectives for a new era.* Thousand Oaks, CA, US: Sage Publications, Inc.

Hoey, J. K. (2017, January). Five networking opportunities hidden in your average workday. *Fast Company.* Retrieved from https://www.fastcompany.com/3067075/five-networking-opportunities-hidden-in-your-average-workday

Kelly, K. (2016). The inevitable: Understanding the 12 technological forces that will shape our future. New York: Viking.

Lieberman, A., and McLaughlin, M. (1992). Networks for educational change: Powerful and problematic. *Phi Delta Kappan,* May, 673–677.

OECD. (2003). *Networks of innovation: Towards new models for managing schools and systems.* Schooling for Tomorrow. Paris: OECD Publishing. Retrieved from https://doi.org/10.1787/9789264100350-en

Renshaw, J. [Jason Renshaw]. (2018, July 28). Innovation is about creating intersections between different domains to see what emerges on the other side. My wife creates these cookies - an intersection of her passion and skills in art and baking. The whole experience of receiving and eating one is quite unique - not at all like eating a regular cookie. [LinkedIn] Retrieved from https://www.linkedin.com/in/jason-renshaw/detail/recent-activity/

Sheninger, E., and Rubin, T. (2017). *BrandED: Tell your story, build relationships and empower learning.* San Francisco, CA: Jossey-Bass.

CHAPTER 5

Clark, D. (2015, April). Why public schools are finally getting savvy about marketing. *Forbes.* Retrieved from https://www.forbes.com/sites/dorieclark/2015/04/27/why-public-schools-are-finally-getting-savvy-about-marketing/#5c0f1aa9437e

Cottom, T. (2018, April 20). Newly named I Promise School principal sets sights on creating model for schools across the country. *The Akron Beacon Journal,* Retrieved from https://www.ohio.com/akron/news/newly-named-i-promise-school-principal-sets-sights-on-creating-model-for-schools-across-the-country

Grant, A. (2014). *Give and take : Why helping others drives our success.* New York: Penguin Books

Kaufmann, H. R., Vrontis, D., Czinkota, M., and Hadiono, A. (2012). Corporate branding and transformational leadership in turbulent times. *Journal of Product and Brand Management,* 21(3), 192–204.

Schawbel, D. (2010). *Me 2.0: 4 steps to building your future.* New York: Kaplan Publishing.

CHAPTER 6

[AASA, The School Superintendents Association]. (2018, February 2). *AASA Leadership Services* [Video file]. Retrieved from https://www.youtube.com/watch?v=3QENh6kKtD8

Casciaro, T., Gino, F., and Kouchaki, M. (2016, May). Learn to love networking. *Harvard Business Review*. Retrieved from https://hbr.org/2016/05/learn-to-love-networking

Llopis, G. (2014, July). Leadership is about enabling the full potential of others. *Forbes Magazine*. Retrieved from https://www.forbes.com/sites/glennllopis/2014/07/29/leadership-is-about-enabling-the-full-potential-in-others/#38cc77c56698

Merchant, B. (2017, September 15). The father of mobile computing is not impressed. *Fast Company*. Retrieved from https://www.fastcompany.com/40435064/what-alan-kay-thinks-about-the-iphone-and-technology-now

Petriglieri, G., Ashford, S.J., & Wrzesniewski, A. (2018, March-April). Thriving in the gig economy. *Harvard Business Review*. Retrieved from https://hbr.org/2018/03/thriving-in-the-gig-economy

CHAPTER 7

Dulworth, M. (2008). *The connect effect: Building strong personal, professional, and virtual networks*. San Francisco, CA: Berrett-Koehler Publishers, Inc.

Farthing, K. (2010). The importance of maintaining a professional network. *Hospital Pharmacy*, 45(8), 592.

Fredricks, S. M. (2003). Creating and maintaining networks among leaders: An exploratory case study of two leadership training programs. *Journal of Leadership and Organizational Studies*, 10(1), 45–54.

Gabriel, J. G., and Farmer, P. C. (2009). *How to help your school thrive without breaking the bank [electronic book]*. Alexandria, Va.: Association for Supervision and Curriculum Development.

Hopkins, D., and Higham, R. (2007). System leadership: Mapping the landscape. *School Leadership and Management*, 27(2), 147–166.

Jarillo, J. C., and Ricart, J. E. (1987). Sustaining networks. *Interfaces*, 17(5), 82–91.

McCarthy, B. (2006). Building and sustaining trust in networks: Lessons from the performing arts. *Irish Marketing Review*, 18(1/2), 47–57.

McIntyre, M. G. (1999). Five ways to turn your management team into a leadership team. *The Journal for Quality and Participation*, 22(4), 40–44.

Sunseri, A., and Kosteva, D. (1992). Career development: Periodic review of qualifications can help executives. *Healthcare Financial Management*, 46(8), 78.

Willem, A., and Lucidarme, S. (2014). Pitfalls and challenges for trust and effectiveness in collaborative networks. *Public Management Review*, 16(5), 733–760.

CHAPTER 8

Battiston, F., Iacovacci, J., Nicosia, V., Bianconi, G., and Latora, V. (2016). Emergence of multiplex communities in collaboration networks. *PLoS ONE*, 11(1), e0147451.

Carson, J. B., Tesluk, P. E., and Marrone, J. A. (2017). Shared leadership in teams: An investigation of antecedent conditions and performance. *Academic of Management Journal*, 50(5), 1217–1234.

Díaz-Gibson, J., Civís-Zaragoza, M., and Guàrdia-Olmos, O. (2014). Strengthening education through collaborative networks: Leading the cultural change. *School Leadership & Management: Formerly School Organisation*, 34(2), 179–200.

Feiock, R., Lee, I., and Park, H. (2012). Administrators and elected officials' collaboration networks: Selecting partners to reduce risk in economic development. *Public Administration Review*, 72(s1), 58–68.

Hopkins, M. M., O'Neil, D. A., Passarelli, A., and Bilimoria, D. (2008). Women's leadership development strategic practices for women and organizations. *Consulting Psychology Journal: Practice and Research*, 60(4), 348-365. doi:http://dx.doi.org.cupdx.idm.oclc.org/10.1037/a0014093

Keller, T., and Dansereau, F. (1995). Leadership and empowerment: A social exchange perspective. *Human Relations*, 48, 127–146.

Martins, E. C., and Terblanche, F. (2003). Building organizational culture that stimulates creativity and innovation. *European Journal of Innovation Management*, 6(1), 64–74.

McIntyre, M. G. (1999). Five ways to turn your management team into a leadership team. *The Journal for Quality and Participation*, 22(4), 40–44.

Mischen, P. A. (2015). Collaborative network capacity. *Public Management Review*, 17(3), 380–403.

Moolenaar, N. M., Sleegers, P. J. C., and Daly, A. J. (2012). Teaming up: Linking collaboration networks, collective efficacy, and student achievement. *Teaching and Teacher Education*, 28, 251–262.

Muijs, D., M. West, and Ainscow, M. 2010. Why network? Theoretical perspectives on networking. *School Effectiveness and School Improvement*, 21(1), 5–26.

Rahman, S. H. A., Endut, I. R., Faisol, N., and Paydar, S. (2014). The importance of collaboration in construction industry from contractors' perspectives. *Procedia-Social and Behavioral Sciences*, 129, 414–421.

Singh, H., Kryscynski, D., Li, X., and Gopal, R. (2016). Pipes, pools and filters: How collaboration networks affect innovative performance. *Strategic Management Journal*, 37(8), 1649–1666.

Spreitzer, G. M. (2017). Social structural characteristics of psychological empowerment. *Academy of Management Journal*, 39(2), 483–504.

Willem, A., and Lucidarme, S. (2014). Pitfalls and challenges for trust and effectiveness in collaborative networks. *Public Management Review*, 16(5), 733–760.

About the Authors

Brian Creasman, EdD, is currently superintendent of Fleming County Schools in Kentucky. His Twitter account says he has the best job in Kentucky. He has served as an assistant superintendent, a high school and middle school principal and assistant principal, and an instructional technologist and classroom teacher. He is the coauthor of *The Leader Within: Understanding and Empowering Teacher Leaders*; *Growing Leaders Within: A Process toward Teacher Leadership*; and *Can Every School Succeed? Bending Constructs to Transform an American Icon*. Brian can be reached at briankcreasman@gmail.com. He can also be found on Twitter at @FCSSuper. He is the co-moderator of #bendingED, the national and international school transformation chat on Twitter.

Bernadine Futrell, PhD, is an experienced educator, who currently serves as the director of Leadership Services for AASA, The School Superintendents Association. She is a contributor to the book *Self-Study Teacher Research: Improving Your Practice through Collaborative Inquiry* (2010). Dr. Futrell is on the Educational Psychology Advisory Board for George Mason University and the Educational Leadership Advisory Board for Howard University. In addition, Dr. Futrell with her husband, former Virginia state delegate Michael Futrell, leads the youth-focused, nonprofit organization, Make the Future. She can be reached at bernadinefutrell@gmail.com or @DrFutrell on Twitter.

Trish Rubin, MA/MPA, is currently a branding/marketing consultant to K-16 education and business clients. Following a K-12 multifaceted career in public education at the local and national levels, Trish Rubin founded NYC-based Trish Rubin Ltd. She is an author and keynote speaker. Her books include *Trish Rubin's New York Minute for Networking* and *BrandED* with Eric Sheninger. She writes for *District Administration* magazine. Trish is an instructor of MBA students in marketing and branding at Baruch College in NYC and at IESEG School of Management in Paris. Reach Trish at www.trishrubin.com. Connect at trishbrand.nyc@gmail.com, @trishrubin on Twitter, @trishrubinnyc on Instagram, and https://www.linkedin.com/in/trishrubinnetworking/.

www.ingramcontent.com/pod-product-compliance
Lightning Source LLC
Chambersburg PA
CBHW030113010526
44116CB00005B/229